LOVE YOUR MOTHER

James Low

Published by Simply Being www.simplybeing.co.uk

British Library Cataloguing in Publication Data. A catalogue record for this book is available from the British Library.

ISBN: 978-1-7399381-8-5

Cover image: Prajnaparamita accessed from the Himalayan Art Resources (https://www.himalayanart.org). Wisdom Publications offers their permission for the use of this image: Deities of Tibetan Buddhism: The Zurich Paintings of the Icons Worthwhile to See (Bris sku mthon ba don ldan). Edited by Martin Wilson and Martin Brauen. Translated by Martin Wilson. Introduced by Martin Brauen. Illustrated by Robert Beer. Wisdom Publications, Boston 2000.

With thanks to Käthe Kollwitz for the use of her drawing of mother and child.

All translations and commentaries by James Low

Prepared by Barbara Terris

Book Layout by Sarah Allen

Contents

Praise to Mother Emptiness

མ་དང་པོ་ལུས་སེམས་སྐྱེད་པའི་མ།

MA	DANG PO	LU	SEM	KYE PAI	MA
mother	*first*	*body*	*mind*	*gave birth to*	*mother*

Mother, at the beginning you were the mother giving birth to me, body and mind.

བར་དུ་ཟང་ཟིང་འབོགས་པའི་མ།

BAR DU	ZANG ZING	BOG PAI	MA
between, *in the middle*	*food, possessions*	*provide*	*mother*

Then you were the mother providing everything I need.

ཐ་མར་སྐྱེ་མེད་སྟོན་པའི་མ།

THA MAR	KYE ME	TON PAI	MA
finally	*unborn,* *emptiness*	*showed*	*mother*

Finally you are the mother showing me my unborn essence.

མ་དྲིན་མོ་ཆེ་ལ་ཕྱག་འཚལ་བསྟོད།།

MA	DRIN MO	CHE	LA	CHAG TSHAL	TOE
mother	*kind*	*great*	*to*	*bow to*	*praise*

I bow to and praise my most kind Mother.

Mother, at the beginning you were the mother giving birth to me, body and mind. Then you were the mother providing everything I need. Finally you are the mother showing me my unborn essence. I bow to and praise my most kind Mother.

Introduction

Where do we come from? This is a profound question that perhaps we do not ask often enough. It seems that all human societies have myths regarding their origins. Some groups believe they came down from the realms of the gods, climbing down a rope. Others believe that a particular god made them. Nowadays we have stories of evolution and the happenstance that allowed some groups to survive and others to vanish. On a more personal level, did I come from somewhere else in order to be born? Am I living in the right place and in the right way now? When I die, will I go somewhere? If so, how will that destination be decided? Such questions can help us to review our assumptions and offer us new perspectives on our lives. However, many of the answers we bring are mere speculations, the fruits of our own thinking and imagining.

In buddhism we are more concerned with questions about our mind. We all have minds for they are the basis of our experiences, such as reading these words. We can learn about our mind by study, but we can also gain direct knowledge of our mind through enquiry. We can question how our mind is in a gentle open way that allows revelation of the actual rather than the evocation of the familiar conceptual. If you look without looking for something, you will see what cannot be seen.

The following five questions are very helpful for meditators who seek direct knowledge. Does the mind have shape or colour? Does it have a size? Does it come from somewhere? Does it abide somewhere? Does it go somewhere? These five questions can also be asked about thoughts, feelings, memories, plans and so on. If we are content to take our everyday experience for granted then we have no need of such questions but sometimes life events shake our complacency and we start to wonder about the actual status of all that we take for granted.

When I was conceived, was this achieved just with matter from my mother and father? Did my mind or soul come from somewhere else? Do I have a soul or is that just a cultural belief? That I have a mind seems undeniable, yet what is my mind? Is it a construct formed of memories, intentions, thoughts, feelings, hopes, fears and so on? Or is it more like a sense of presence, an availability open to experience?

This short book points out a buddhist way of attending to such questions. If we wish to see and know the actual truth of how we are then we have to question all our beliefs and assumptions. What is the basis of my existence? By reflecting and inquiring, we come to see the transience of much that we rely on. Since the contents of my experiences are transient, what do I consist of? Is there any basis for believing that I exist? I am here, in this environment, breathing in and out – but do I exist? Do I have an inherent existence or only a contingent identity? We need to loosen the topsoil we stand on and see if there is an actual enduring basis to how we take ourselves to be. Such enquiry can help us see that our sense of ourselves is built on sand, on a flow of moments. However, despite this impermanence, here we are, present in every stage of our life. This presence has no substance and yet it endures – how strange!

This is the mystery of emptiness, that the empty essence of all that appears is inseparable from each and every appearance. Moreover, our own mind is empty of self-substance yet bright with ceaseless movement. The fact that our mind has no substantial basis is not a lack. In fact, emptiness is the site of the emergent qualities of every occurrence.

Until we directly awaken to its actuality, 'emptiness' is merely a useful concept for guiding us towards seeing the absence of inherent existence in both people and all sentient beings, as well as in all phenomena. THE HEART SUTRA points out that emptiness is not a separate entity, nor even an ethereal one. The transient collection of the five constituents of our sense of self is itself empty of inherent existence. Our form, feelings, perceptions, associations and consciousnesses all arise as dependent arisings. None exists all by itself. The transient collection of the aggregates is a traditional Buddhist way of thinking about what constitutes a person. I am keeping to this way of analysing personhood but it may not mean much to you. So please take the time to write down and consider all the factors making you who you take yourself to be. Then look at them in the following way.

In this usage, the term 'self' indicates the nature of things which do not depend on another. Such entities as 'my self', 'my house', 'this dog', do not exist in themselves, out of themselves, as themselves. They are all dependent on and arise from and with the appearance of other transient causal factors, each of which rests on its own network of causal factors. It is our own use of concepts which marks the boundaries of entities which we take to be separate and autonomous. If we examine any 'thing' at all, we will see its dependent interconnectivity with other 'things'. In fact, the field of our experience is inherently undivided—its divisions only appear to exist when seen through the distorting lens of reification and duality. Thus the field and all that arises within the field is selfless as the infinite variety of the non-duality of appearance and emptiness.

To help our own practice, we can focus on the view of emptiness of a person, seeing that what we take them to be — a person — is a dynamic of cause and effect. If this is clear, then seeing the emptiness of phenomena is easier. This is because if the emptiness of the subject, the person, is clear, then the emptiness of the object becomes apparent and the delusion of duality dissolves.

All the faults of the afflictions arise from taking the transient collection or skandhas to be a real self. The key afflictions are assumption, attraction, aversion, pride, and jealousy, with the first, the assumption that self has inherent existence, being their common foundational delusion. The five aspects of the transient collection — form, feeling, perception, associations, and consciousness — are taken to constitute or be a real self which has the nominally existent 'I' as its support or object. 'I' functions as both the referring subject (I like this tea) and the referent object (I am angry with myself).

The great Indian philosopher Nagarjuna states in verse 35 of his Precious Garland: *As long as there is a conception of the mental and physical aggregates (as inherently existent), just so long is there a conception of an 'I' (as inherently existent). When the conception of an 'I' exists, there is (dualistic) action. From (dualistic) action there arises birth.*

Self is a delusion arising from ignoring dependent arising. Thus a person's complacent abiding as if able to establish themselves in their own right without being imputed by thought is called the belief in 'self' or inherent existence. The self, our self, has no inherent existence, yet here we are! We appear and so are not nothing at all. Yet our appearance depends on so many transient factors. We are neither mere nothingness nor eternal. The truth of our situation is the middle way free of all extremes. To see that our 'existence' is not inherent but merely imputed is to overcome our innate tendency to take the false appearance of the 'I' as if inherently existent. This reveals the basis of its designation as a real existent to be false and without true foundation. If dependent arising is seen, ignorance does not arise. Through conquering ignorance, all afflictions are conquered. Ignorance, which is the conception of inherent existence, is the root of the tree of samsara. If the root is truly cut, all the leaves and branches will wither.

All our experiences are formulated through our belief that the transitory collection constitutes a real self. Moreover, the nominally existent 'I' is the object or point of reference for all the constituents of our delusional self. It is vital to truly investigate our own situation so that the Dharma teachings are not mere words, but become a lamp that illuminates the illusory nature of the self. Belief in an inherently existent self is the key obstacle to awakening: it is the enemy that has to be defeated. Therefore, we need to see that the 'I' is only designated to the body and mind which are its bases of designation. Since body and mind arise dependently, there is no actual basis of designation. 'I' is an empty signifier without a real referent. Neither 'I' nor its presumed referent has inherent existence.

The mind thinking of 'I' exists in our mental continuum, whether waking or sleeping, and influences all our experience although it can seem invisible due to being taken for granted. When we have an intense experience of happiness or sadness our sense of 'I' is increased. So, whether with an actual situation or with a remembered or imagined one in which you are excited or afraid, very happy or very sad, use the opportunity to examine the 'I' which seems to be the object or recipient of the pleasing or provocative event. The intensity of the manifest mind thinking 'I' makes it foreground and you should let it intensify. Then the way that the mind conceives the 'I' should be investigated. This should be done gently, otherwise the looker will cause the looked at to vanish. Keep the focus on the recognition of 'I' and only secondarily on the qualities it seems to have. Here we rest in calm abiding shamatha and allow our focused attention to settle on 'I'. Maintain this, while also giving a little attention to how 'I' is being apprehended and conceived.

With this we move from the sense that the 'I' of the thought 'I' seems to exist in the centre of the heart to starting to analyse how the 'I' is. Sometimes it may appear to be related to the body and sometimes it may seem to be related to the mind or to be related with the other aggregates such as feelings, perceptions and associations. Seeing that the objects related to can vary, yet 'I' continues, you come to identify an 'I' that exists inherently in its own right. This 'I' is unaltered by what it is related to and is from the beginning established in and by itself. Now you have ascertained the 'I' as the object which has to be negated by seeing its selflessness. You have identified the 'I', conceived by the inborn conceiver of an 'I', as self-established, and as having a relation with your own aggregates, like that of water poured into water.

This 'I' must be identified in this way, otherwise you will not be able to identify it as having non-inherent existence. The basis of designation, of identification, is the aggregates, while the phenomenon designated is 'I', which is inherently self-established in relation to the five aggregates. If the 'I' exists, it is either one with, or separate from, the aggregates. In either case, they pervade or occur with every instance of an existent 'I'.

If 'I' is one with the body, it would not be sensible to say 'my body' from the point of view of affixing an attribute, 'body', to a base, 'I'. Examine to see if this is the same if 'I' were one with the mind. As Nagarjuna says, "*When it is taken that there is no self except the aggregates, the appropriated aggregates themselves are the self. If so, your self is non-existent.*" If the 'I' and the aggregates are inherently one there would be no difference between the appropriator 'I' and the five aggregates which are appropriated by it.

As Chandrakirti, says, "*If this self were the aggregates, then because there are many, those selves would also be many.*" If this were the case, then on whom would your actions of a former life ripen? Again, Chandrakirti says, "*There is no self other than the aggregates because apart from the aggregates, its conception does not exist.*" This has to be investigated until you gain a clear conviction. Chandrakirti says, "*Because there is no object which does not have an agent, there is no 'mine' (owned) without a self (owner). Through the view of emptiness of 'I' and 'mine', a yogi is liberated.*"

With equipoise achieved through calm abiding, the appearance of the mere nominality of an 'I' arises like a magician's illusion in place of the former belief in an inherently existing 'I'. As Chandrakirti says, "*Those objects which are apprehended by the world with the six faultless senses are truths just for the world."* There is no contradiction between ultimate absolute truth and relative or conventional truth.

The mahayana vision of the Three Doors to Liberation can help us to stabilise our practice. They are emptiness, signlessness and wishlessness. The recognition of emptiness refers to correctly apprehending that the basis of the aggregates, elements and sense fields is not real or permanent. The recognition of signlessness or the absence of characteristics means that there is no conceptual identification of perceptions. The recognition of wishlessness refers to the absence of reliance on conceptual aims and goals.

The stability of mind that understands analytically that all dharmas are empty of their own mark is the emptiness gateway to liberation.

The stability of mind that understands analytically that all dharmas are without a causal sign is the signless gateway to liberation.

The stability of mind that understands analytically that all dharmas do not occasion anything is the wishless gateway to liberation.

However these three doors can be blocked by incorrect perception.

Perceiving the basis as real blocks the gateway of emptiness.

Believing the path to have real characteristics blocks the gateway to absence of characteristics.

Considering the result as something to be wished for blocks the gateway to wishlessness.

A direct awakening to emptiness as the basis brings a dropping of any clinging to either path or result.

There are three sections to this book: Love your Mother; Dependent Arising; and Awakening to Emptiness: the Heart Sutra. The first section explores our origins and uses the clarity that arises from this to ease us out of our isolation.

To love your mother is to feel the gratitude that dissolves the ego-self. In this life we were developed in our mother's body and then were birthed by her. We should remember this. She fed us, cleaned us, helped us to speak and to learn to function in the world. Later this mothering function was carried on by teachers, friends, employers— they taught us our cultural beliefs. Then, if we are fortunate, we meet our mother-guru who shows us our mind as it is. With this we find ourselves opening to the open, to the great emptiness, our primordial ground. The first mother builds us up, while the guru-mother shows us the translucency of all constructs. Moreover, all beings have been our mother in previous lives and have done so much for our welfare. Gratitude softens our defended delusion of independence so that we can see that we are truly part of the whole. To be a self that considers itself to be self-existing is to be apart from all that is other than that self. This is the prison of isolation and separation. Love your mother! Indeed, please do love your mother. Releasing your resistance to this will set you free.

On a relative level, loving our mother and all our past mothers arouses and strengthens our wish to work for the benefit of all sentient beings. We have a debt of gratitude which we should repay. On a deeper level, our mother guru shows us the emptiness of our mind. We do not exist as a thing. We are the manifest presence of the ground. We have always actually been the manifest presence of the ground, yet we did not see this. Without the kindness of the mother guru this awakening would not happen. This is a kindness that cannot be repaid—except by abiding in openness and showing this truth to others. This first section shows us how to become familiar with the ground, our true infinite mother.

The second section describes how we wander in samsara due to the dependent arising of the twelve links on the wheel of becoming. Our tendency to see objects and people as real existents is very powerful. By reifying ourselves and all others and all appearances we bring a false sense of stability to our dynamic, interactive, ever-changing life. When we examine our circumstances through the lens of dependent arising we see that each moment arises on the basis of the previous moment. The appearances we took to be autonomous entities are in fact part of the chain of becoming. They each arise on the basis of something other than themselves and in turn become the basis of the arising of something else. Not one single atom of independent existence can be found anywhere.

If we can apply this understanding in our daily life, then we start to see the illusory nature of our experience. Neither we nor anyone else has an enduring self-substance. We appear, yet we do not exist as something. Our appearance manifests like a dream image or a mirage. There is nothing to hold on to, and so our habit of grasping and clinging is revealed to be an unnecessary and rather foolish waste of time. Now we can relax because we sense that we are an illusion amongst illusions.

The third section describes how we can use the teaching of the HEART SUTRA to awaken to emptiness. All occurrences are empty of self. They have no inherent existence. In this way all 'things' are not things, for they lack separate existence. We live in a vast field of interconnectivity – all appearances are linked to other appearances. They are inseparable from emptiness. We have to be careful not to turn emptiness into a subtle metaphysical substance – it is not. What it is and how it is cannot be asserted. It escapes every definition and every momentary insight and yet it is present with everything that we experience. This is a great mystery to which we have to respectfully seek entrance. It is not a problem for the rational mind to solve. We are inseparable from emptiness. We are apparitions, beings of light. Emptiness is our mother. The mother we come from, live within and never leave. We are the radiance of emptiness. May we open to the ever-open!

May the texts in this book liberate you from the fetters of duality!

Love Your Mother

C. R. Lama
manifest union
of
the Wisdom of the Mother
&
the Kindness of the Father

EXPLORING THE CAUSE: OUR POTENTIAL FOR AWAKENING

Love your mother! We have our mother who gave birth to us and the possibility of life; this is a woman who was also a partner and a daughter, a worker, a woman with many, many different identities. We often have quite complicated relations with our mother. However in Mahayana Buddhism we are concerned with emptiness as our true mother. She is the mother of all the buddhas, and we find our own buddhahood or enlightenment through her. By entering into the womb of emptiness we awaken to the truth of who we are and how this world is. In buddhism we find many different levels of understanding offered to us. From the levels of higher tantra and dzogchen we have never been apart from this mother, and she has already given birth to us without giving birth to anything. She is ceaselessly giving non-birth to us, and in this way she is the blessing or gift of the deconstruction of the delusion of an individual self.

Tibetan Buddhism offers us the vehicles or approaches of the cause and the vehicles or approaches of the result. We will begin by looking at the cause which is the potential we all have for awakening. At the moment this potential is covered with various obscurations. Due to this it seems hidden from us, and therefore we have to make effort to find it. Spiritual life is presented as a journey towards enlightenment which is to be found somewhere else. As long as we believe in the truth of our individual separate identity, this is the only possibility open to us. Believing that we are our sense of separate existence we have to find the way towards that which is not separated from emptiness.

Prajnaparamita, transcendent wisdom, is the mother of all the buddhas while Avalokiteshvara, the presence of loving kindness, is the father of all the buddhas. It is their inseparability that will guide us on the path. Without the mother, emptiness, the method of connectivity, compassion can become the energy of the ego-self. Most sentient beings take care of their own children and help their friends. They manifest some kind of care and concern. Yet even if this has an altruistic flavour, even if it seems to be truly for the other, because the ones I help are part of my area of concern, at least some of my intention is self-referential. C. R. Lama often said that there is no virtue in the family. That is to say, if parents feed their children and try to keep them safe, this is not a great virtue. But if you feed a stranger, if you take care of an orphan, then it becomes virtuous, and it becomes virtuous not just towards the orphan but towards yourself. When you are truly kind to someone else, with no obligation or duty enforcing it, you are stepping out of the enclosed circle of 'me first'. Genuine kindness towards the other will always help to dissolve the sense of being a separate individual self. In parallel with this, by seeing the emptiness of all things we see that they are not actually divided, and through this we can experience interconnectivity. This connectivity is the quality of kindness. If you go fully into emptiness you find yourself with kindness and if you go fully into kindness you find yourself with emptiness.

In buddhism our strong belief in the separate reality of the phenomena around us and of ourselves is described as mental dullness, an opacity which hides the bright truth of interconnectivity in emptiness. Unfortunately we are all caught up in this dullness most of the time. When we see an object as existing in itself, and we see ourselves as a subject entity existing in itself, then we find ourselves trying to work out where we stand with this thing: do we like it, do we want it, do we need it. Or perhaps we are a little afraid of it, feeling some dislike for it and wishing for it to be far away. It could also be that we are just indifferent, we don't care, and the object means nothing to us. Even with this last positioning there is still a confirmation of our separate self. When we walk down the street we take the pavement for granted. We don't pay attention to the fact that there is a pavement. We don't say a prayer for the workers who made the pavement or for the council who repairs it. This indifference frees us to be in our own thoughts and this self-involvement confirms our own individual identity. If we can take the shape of the world for granted, then we have more time to spend on ourselves.

In order to interrupt this self-absorption, in the buddhist tradition we look at the six realms, the six possible environments in which sentient life is to be found. The texts remind us that although there is endless pleasure in some of the god realms, if you want to practise dharma you're better off with a human life. This is because in the human realm you get some happiness and some sorrow. You expand on a happy day and shrink back on a sad day. If we observe this in ourselves it helps us to see that we are linked with the environment. Although we think of ourselves as separate and individual, we are so very sensitive that we react to the shaping of another person's face, whether they smile or frown when they see us.

At this time we have a precious human birth where we can easily experience the impermanence of outer phenomena and of our own moods, thoughts and sensations. I am not a stable isolate, I am not a fixed entity. My life is based on ceaseless interaction with the environment. In fact it is not that I am surrounded by the environment but rather that I am an inextricable aspect of the environment and I change with it. Hence I am unreliable, I am unpredictable. Moreover, because the world is revealed to me through my own capacity for perception and interpretation, how I am influences how the world is for me. When we start to practise we feel ourselves to be inside our skin bag, looking out at the world. The seeming solidity and separateness of the forms around us promotes the opacity of our deluded dualistic perception. The more separate we see them to be the more they become a barrier to our insight. We are actively involved in the unfolding of our experience, and our life is an ongoing relationship or conversation with the environment. For example, in England the harvest for the main crops is over and now we have a lot of rain. This is not so bad for the farmers but it is not great for me because I prefer the sun. The value of the rain is not something neutral. All phenomena are revealed to us through interpretation. We live in stories and we are always part of these stories. How I look, how I hear, how I touch – all my ways of entering into these interactions are co-emergent with the quality of what is arising.

If we can see this then we start to discern the basis for awakening or enlightenment or liberation. The site of revelation or the site of disclosure of our unchanging original buddha nature is here with us always. The more we allow ourselves to be present moment by moment with the unborn emergent, we awaken to the inseparability of the ever-pure openness and the ceaseless immediacy of its non-dual radiance. Abiding with the intrinsic perfection of each moment, we relax and free ourselves from the delusion that our ego-identity could in any way improve the always already complete and perfect. Relaxing into the openness of the source, the need to maintain the delusion of identity self-liberates. We are the apparitional flowering of the potential of the groundless ground, the inexhaustible source.

Samsara, this experience of wandering on, going from one situation to another, one stage of our life to another, arises from ignorance. That is to say we don't see the simple actuality of how it is. Instead, we imagine how it is. We suffer from an excess of mental activity as all the thoughts, feelings, memories that arise for us seem to be expressions of ourself. 'I am the thinker of my thoughts.' This belief is shared by most human beings and so its falsity is unexamined. Due to this we are unable to directly see either the ground of the mental activity or the actual quality of mental activity. We reify thoughts, feelings, memories, plans, and interpretations of people, places and so on so that our experience is composed and crafted rather than simple and spontaneous. That is to say, we take these subtle traces of experience which have already vanished and use them to build up our stable predictive interpretation. And then we live inside the belief that that interpretation captures the truth of the situation.

When a baby is very small it doesn't have much recognition of the people around. Its recognition tends to be in terms of the smell of the mother, the taste of the milk and so on. But as the months proceed they start to have more sense of 'this is my mum', this is somebody who is there and who, if I cry, will come and take care of me. Then when this small person is first able to say 'mum', it is like the royal seal on a Charter: whatever this woman thinks she is, she is now further sealed inside 'mum'. Because she is simply my mum, I, the child, don't need to think about it; it is manifest, this is how she is, this is what she is. I might see her with my dad if he's around, or with siblings or wider family, or see her talking with friends, but certainly when I'm small, four and five years of age, I know that if I say 'mum' loudly enough I will pull her out of the false identities they attribute to her. That is to say I am committed to my blinkered identification in order to maintain the reassuring certainty that this woman is just my mum, wholly my mum. I blind myself to all the other evidence which indicates she is a complex polyvocal person. I'm living inside my assumption. I assume that my mother will always know where my socks are, and she will know what I'm doing in school tomorrow and what I have to take. I'm taking her as an extension of myself.

We can take this as a metaphor for our situation in samsara: I take myself to be a human being, I perceive the world around me in terms of my own embodiment. This is how it is. I'm just me and as far as I can remember I've always been me. There are birds and there are fish and there are dogs and cats and they do what they do: they are not like me! I am as I am and all these things just are as they are. This is the starting point for most of us when we come in contact with buddhist dharma, and we are not even conscious that we are cocooned in such limiting beliefs.

In order to give ourselves a fresh perspective with which we might put our assumptions into question, dharma highlights the importance of wisdom and compassion. In order to develop wisdom we consider impermanence, dependent origination and the absence of inherent existence. In order to develop kindness we consider the suffering that all living creatures have to face. We develop a positive attitude towards them, wishing them well: may all sentient beings be happy, may fish be happy, may crows be happy, and cows too, may all the many different kinds of creatures be happy. The true basis of their happiness is that they have the possibility of awakening. The cow is not essentially a cow for it has buddha nature. However, contingently, due to causes and circumstances this ever-present potential for awakening is hidden by the cow's defining experience of enacting 'cow-ness' even if this is not conceptualised. What we would call the cow's instinctive cow-ness is in fact the ripening of a pattern of karma. It is the same with fish, and of course it is the same with us.

We think that we are a human being, and that this is our enduring definitive identity. Even if we know that we are going to die, it often does not feel that way. The felt sense that, 'I am just me', seems to have no beginning and so why would it have an end? Those religions that say, 'oh, you can go up to heaven where you will still be like a human being', offer another kind of continuity – everything may change around me, and I may die, yet I will still be sentient as I, me, myself. Buddhism, however, is saying something much more radical: what you take to be yourself is an appearance, appearing and changing along with all other appearances. It is not resting on some essential human beingness. We manifest as human beings due to specific patterns of causes and conditions. When these causes and conditions alter, your life in human form ends and new patterns of causes and conditions bring about new manifestations. There is no essential 'you' travelling from one life to the next. The relative potential supporting this life dissolves into nothingness and then the potential of nothingness manifests according to the karmic potential available and a new life occurs as a fresh experience. There is no fixed self that passes from one life to another.

What we call the 'self' is not a fixed entity. Our self is the site of the activity of manifesting different moods, thoughts, feelings and so on moment by moment. This display of the potential for 'selfing' is inseparable from emptiness. No one single moment of self-formation has inherent existence. We are the ceaseless display of emptiness. We are ungraspable and limitless – although when we identify with concepts about ourselves we delude ourselves with the falsifying belief that we are knowable entities. Whether I experience myself to be thoughtful or distracted, happy or sad, these are not aspects of who I actually am, they're not like adjectives and adverbs giving some information about the eternal noun of I, me, myself. Rather they are the flourishing of a potential which is not defined by the illusory patterns of its flourishing. It is activity per se, the movement of the mind, which gives rise to our fleeting formations. All the forms of samsara arise from activity. Karma is the word most commonly used to refer to this activity. The formulating quality of karmic activity is the mind deluded by the belief in duality. Due to this, subject and object and their connection are each taken to be real and substantial. On the basis of my belief that there is a definite object with true qualities, I develop an intention towards it. This intention is usually inflected by the affect of liking or disliking, of jealousy and so on. This emotional content is the energising force which takes us into the activity of connection with the other person or thing. Our intention could be life enhancing or destructive for the other.

The basis for our involved activity is the dualistic view that subject and object are separate real entities. This delusion arises from ignorance which is not a state but an activity. It is the activity of ignoring the ever-open ground of everything. From this arises 'selfing', which is also not a state but an activity of identifying diverse factors and patterns as if they were a continuous stable 'self'. By not seeing how I actually am, I am not in touch with my absence of inherent existence. Due to this I take the terms I, me, myself to refer to my own existence as this someone: I think, 'I'm just me.' Within the unquestioned belief in duality it seems obvious the 'me' refers to my enduring existence and that the defining essence of me is my own felt sense that 'here I am.' But this 'me' is actually just an idea. Due to believing in this idea I cling to my existence as basic, the given root of my life. Although I experience my life as changing: the flow of perceptions and judgement, of sensations, feelings, thoughts, memories and so on, this actual experience rarely puts my belief in my enduring existence as someone into question. Our ordinary dualistic perception seems quite reasonable: I want to know where my shoes are. I am confident that I am the owner of shoes, and I need to go out so where are my shoes? I am entitled to own shoes and therefore I'm entitled to be upset if you take away my shoes.

This is the basis of law: that the world is constructed out of things which can be defined and refined as commodities which can be owned. You can own land. A country can own the airspace above it, it can try to own the entitlement to fish in the waters around it. In many cultures people are entitled to own other people as slaves or bonded labourers. In very patriarchal cultures the senior male seems to own the whole family and in particular the women. So we're very, very used to swimming in a sea of things where I, the swimmer, am also a thing. So, the first point that we need to clarify if we are going to approach true discernment or wisdom is whether entities actually exist. To do this we study impermanence. We look at the outer forms of change, the seasons and so on. We examine impermanence in relation to our body: we get older, we're not able to do the things we did when we were very young. We note that we like different foods at different times of the year. Although you might have a favourite food and say that you love it, if you had to have it three times a day every day, you might change your mind.

This indicates that my relation with my body and with the world around me is thought-mediated. So my idea about strawberry ice cream is not the same as eating a huge amount of strawberry ice cream. In the realm of ideas I love strawberry ice cream, but if I have to eat a two-kilo tub of ice cream, then I'm going to feel very sick, and towards the end this ice cream is not going to be so interesting. That is because I have a different relationship with the idea of strawberry ice cream from the actuality of eating a lot of it. We can maintain a positive relationship with our idea of someone or something even when we experience negative feelings about them.

The idea of what we take the object to be is not the same as the actuality of interactive connectivity with the phenomena. The somethingness of the object, its apprehendability is an idea. The actual phenomena is an appearing, a fleeting presence. It is not the appearance of something. Phenomena are only available in this moment. When you consider the future, you are using ideas to imagine what is not here. When you think of the past you are evoking transient mental images. Phenomena are always now. Ideas move across the linked three times of past, present and future. The present embedded in the three times is not the open actual present; it is a conceptual present. So, if a mother asks a child: "What are you doing now?" The reply, "I'm reading my book!" is a lie in terms of the actual phenomenology. They are talking about the past, about what they were doing. By her question the mother has taken the child out of where they were. If the child were to tell the truth of the actual, they would say, "I am talking with you." But the mother might well take that as rudeness. The question which interrupts the immersed present is requesting an answer referring to something nameable. The activity which was occurring in linear time is not an idea, yet we can only refer to it by talking about something which has been displaced into the past by the need to reply in the fleeting present. The actual present is uncatchable and indescribable in thought or speech. It is manifest yet elusive.

When you examine this kind of experience for yourself, you see the power of concepts embedded in language to generate a world of interpretation which is taken to be equivalent to the world of phenomena but is not. Phenomena are immediately presenting and rapidly fleeting whereas concepts conjure up the sense of events as apprehendable entities. When I am talking, I am talking about something, something which you and I have to believe is existing in order for our communication to be meaningful. The illusory yet seemingly graspable conceptualised 'entity' becomes the object of our attention as it empowers the ego-self to see itself as an active agent, doing and making. Whereas the immediacy of the fleetingly present phenomena which is our actual naked experience has little value for the ego-self and so is largely ignored. This ignoring of the actual in favour of believing the imagined gives rise to all the experiences of samsara. This ignoring of the actual is the mother of samsara while the imagining of the illusory as real is the father of samsara. The intercourse between this perverse mother and father gives rise to the ceaseless flow of our reassuring assumptions about who we are and where we are and what we're going to do. So we have to recognize the power of this misleading mother and father and how generation to generation there is the transmission of the mental dullness which takes our human situation to be a given. We are sent to school, and from our elders we learn about how our culture is and how we should behave. This lineage of dullness and obscuration is not something fixed. It is a dynamic flow of interpreted experiences, each underpinned by the deep mother of ignoring the simple actuality of existence. So, in the time we have together, we're going to focus on finding our true mother, emptiness, the mother of all the buddhas. When we find our true mother, we will also find our true father, the ceaseless display of awareness inseparable from emptiness.

TRUST YOUR MOTHER: RELAX INTO THE OPEN EMPTY SPACE OF AWARENESS

If we keep to the image of the mother, imagine that you are a shy and troubled teenager, and you like to spend your time in your bedroom. Mum comes and knocks on the door and says, "Come on, come, be with us, life is better outside." This is the basis of meditation. When we sit and get distracted, we fall into our little bedrooms, our habitual thoughts, our preoccupations. The teaching says the mind is open, awareness is like the sky, come out, be present in the space you are already part of. Yet somehow our ego-self would rather hide in our thoughts, and our memories are very cosy. So when in the practice you get distracted or caught up in something which is arising, simply remember that your bedroom is inside the flat; it is not a separate world. The flat is in the town and the town is in the big world which is in the sky. So, without blaming yourself, without being critical, just relax back into the open space where transient experiences are arising and passing. So sit, relax, release and let whatever comes come, and let it go. Without involvement, stay with the space, the empty open space of your mind that is your mother. Mum will keep you safe, but these thoughts, they're going to lead you into trouble, trust your mama …

11

Our practice is to relax into the open presence of awareness. This is not something that we can do by effort. Our mind itself is unborn and unchanging, without fixed qualities by which it can be known. Within this openness experiences arise unceasingly. The non-duality of these aspects of stillness and movement is the basis for freedom from grasping at entities. Yet if the open presence of awareness is not opened to, then the activity of the mind is mistaken as the dualistic consciousness of subject and object. The interaction of self and other continues all the time. We are conscious of memory, sensations, outer colours and shapes and so on. Although we take it that we are experiencing 'things', these 'things' are mere moments devoid of fixed essence. Experiences come and go. We experience experiences; we don't experience things. The 'thingness' of things is the misinterpretation of the ephemeral actuality of phenomena. What remains, what abides, are not things, not entities. They are an illusion. What abides is awareness itself, and our awareness, our basic noetic or knowing capacity has no shape or form. It is present yet ungraspable, just like space. Open and present, awareness is always available – but not as an entity or an object for mental interpretations.

In the practice we simply relax and release the dualistic polarities of subject and object. Free of the delusion of being a subject, a separate ego, we open to our own open ground. This open ground is without beginning or end, top or bottom. It is the whole, the infinite, the undivided. It is the sole source. With this clarity we are open and present as experience occurs. There is seeing, hearing, sensing, thinking, remembering. There is no end to experience. Let it be … self-arising and self-vanishing. Stay relaxed in the clarity which is forever uninvolved. Some arisings seem to be 'I, me, myself' whereas others seem to be not-me. Whatever occurs, let it go. The mind is complete in its openness and has nothing to gain or lose through the presence or absence of thoughts. All that I take to be me is vanishing. When we see that directly, free of the false stasis of conceptualisation, then we truly awaken to the illusory dream-like nature of life. Free of the polarities of existence and non-existence, we abide in the non-separation of awareness and emptiness, clarity and emptiness, appearance and emptiness.

Our subjective sense of self is a false identity, just as the habit of ignoring is our false mother. Our habit of identification with moments of consciousness, as if they indicated a permanent self, is the false child. No self has been born. All that is taken to be self is both fleeting and without inherent existence. The mind is empty and it is simultaneously full of unborn, ungraspable experiences. The basis for the rich variety of experience is the ever-changing display of the potential of the ground. Not one atom of 'real' or 'independent' existence has ever occurred.

Dualistic consciousness is deluded and deluding. Subject and object arise together as interpretations of the ever-open field of occurrence. They pulse together, subject enlivening object and object enlivening subject. Moving together they are movement, movement in the non-dual display of movement, of occurrence. Not for one second do they settle – and that is why life within the delusion of duality is so unsettling. The subject is not to be rejected nor to be merged with – it is the play of your own open empty mind and it is the energy of connectivity, the basic kindness of the emergent field in which all appearance is kin.

If you can believe in a film in the cinema, if you can believe in the characters in the novel, then you can start to see that you believe in a self in the same way that you believe in superman. When something is clearly created and artificial we can see through it. But when it is created and believed in, then it can appear to us to be intrinsic. Superman exists, of course he does, as an idea we are taken in by. When we take ideas to be real, this something is born from the deluding mother of ignorance.

Since all that you experience, whether external perceptions or thoughts or feelings, simply arises and passes, these momentary events cannot fulfil your yearning for fulfilment, for peace and enduring happiness. The ego cannot stabilise itself or its situation. It is always reaching forward in the hope of a better future or pulled back by memories, both good and bad. If we wish for awakening, enlightenment, liberation and true freedom, we have to look in the right place which is the non-conceptual here and now. Yet we, the ego-self, are always looking in the wrong place (somewhere else), and we're looking from the wrong position (as a separate self). All places and people are movements of energy in the open field of awareness. This is not a dogma that you're being asked to believe in. You can observe it directly in meditation, but also through reflection on your own experience in daily life. Since you got up this morning, not only have you experienced many object formations, many things arising for you, but you, the experiencer, have manifested as many different formations. Think of the thoughts and feelings that have arisen for you today. Observe how you have believed in them as they occurred, identifying with them as being indicative of you in that moment. I feel happy, I feel sad … this seems to be the truth of me, and then … it vanishes. Through this you can start to see for yourself that your mind itself is empty of its own content. It is an availability which allows the richness of experience to come and go. In this way we are using the fact of impermanence as a lens through which to perceive the ever-changing details of the phenomena that you misconstrue through reliance on concepts. By looking with fresh eyes you can start to see how life is, rather than just believing in your assumptions about it. Now you notice that what you have taken to be fixed and reliable is in fact without its own essence or inherent existence. Like clouds in the sky, all that is taken to be self and other is empty appearances passing by.

DEPENDENT ORIGINATION: THE ABSENCE OF INHERENT EXISTENCE

The dharma also points to the truth of dependent origination, the simple fact that on the basis of this having occurred that will occur. For example, you are alive because you are breathing. On the basis of breathing in you breathe out; on the basis of breathing out you breathe in. We have the words exhale and inhale which seem to indicate two different and distinct functions; there is exhaling and inhaling and they are quite separate. But this kind of conceptualisation is a violence towards the dynamic pulsation of life. These names, and the concepts we can build on them, act as a kind of haze or veil in the mind, creating the delusion of separate independent activities. Breathing is the pulsation of exhaling and inhaling. These movements feed each other, they are linked, interdependent. When you look around your home, you see your furniture which other people have made. Your furniture arises for you on the basis of how much money you have, your taste, the kind of items that you're aware of and on the skills of the crafts-people who make them. Moreover their availability rests on the discussion of the owner of the company and the accountant as to whether their current styles are profitable enough. With this approach we can investigate   everything we encounter and see that each and every item we identify is there because of factors outside its 'self'. This allows us to develop a dynamic view of manifestation arising in interdependence, rather than a perception of enduring isolated entities. You look in the fridge and on the basis of there being nothing there, you go to the shops, then on the basis of shopping you fill the fridge, then on the basis of eating you gradually empty the fridge; so everything, both self and other, is linked together.

For meditators, it is very helpful to keep investigating self and environment, history, geography and every aspect of knowledge until you are personally clear that there are no independent entities. The Theravada view establishes that there is an absence of inherent existence in persons and the mahayana view establishes that there is an absence of inherent existence in phenomena. From the largest phenomena to the very smallest, not one thing appears by itself. If we stop breathing our life will not survive. My life, my existence as me is dependent. If the climate gets very hot, I'm going to die; if it gets very, very cold, I'm going to die. If there is a lot of air pollution around, this will affect my lifespan. There are many, many factors which operate together to give me the sense that I exist. 'I exist' is a conclusion based on this compounded existence not being seen accurately. Because, I can say, 'I am James', it is as if I am an enduring entity, a referent referred to as 'James'. Yet I am James on the basis of breathing and eating and sleeping and walking and talking and studying and going to the toilet. There's no end to the list of factors I would need to include in the composition of me. So it is not that I am just James all by myself, but James is the name given to this specific expression of the interaction of dynamic factors beyond enumeration. My presence as James, or rather the possibility of continuing to refer to these linked yet ever-varying manifestations as 'James' depends on the movement of all these causal factors and maintenance factors, and the absence of the factors of destruction. This kind of analysis is very helpful in exposing how easy it is to become stupid. We are embedded in the stupidity of reification.

For example, if you were in the nyingmapa tradition, you might say that the previous form of Dudjom Rinpoche was a great meditator. You look at a photo of him and say, "What an amazing man!" People talk this way yet it is a sign of confusion. Dudjom Rinpoche was the nirmanakaya of the buddha and as such was not a 'human being'. He showed the form of a man but this was an illusory form, not a reified form. He was ungraspable, yet we can put him in a box and then stack up the boxes. Dudjom Rinpoche is on the top, and then perhaps Chatral Rinpoche, and then Kangyur Rinpoche, and so on until you have a hierarchy of lamas. To make the lama something that can be known and measured is to close the door to liberation. You have reduced the guru to a thing, a commodity. This young Karmapa is amazing! Wonderful! Who is wonderful? The Karmapa. You don't know? Here look, look at the photo, look, he's amazing! Once again you have reification, you're grasping at the representation in the photo as if it was the truth of a person. Yet the Karmapa is an illusory form, an apparition from the heart of the Buddha.

So, if we wish to practise the pure dharma we have to be careful how we think and talk about 'things'. This is because how we think about things is how we make things. The absence of inherent existence means that our existence is conditional and relational. When the Buddha Shakyamuni was enlightened, he did not want to teach anything. He said, what's the point, nobody is going to understand. But various gods came and they asked him again and again and they scattered, and eventually he said, okay. Yet he was still doubtful if the teachings would bring clarity since sentient beings are so fond of confusion. The very act of trying to understand can veil the present moment in veils of assumption and erroneous belief. Dharma manifests because of the wishes of devoted beings. The teaching arises because of requests. The quality of a relationship between teacher and student creates an open or veiled field in which transmission or non-connection occurs. There needs to be an unobscured meeting of the potential for showing and the potential of receiving.

On the basis of the longing of the heart, the clouds of obscuration thin and the pure form of the teacher appears. The more we are sealed in the cocoon of our self-referential ego identity the more we are trapped in the delusion of individualism. If I believe that my life belongs to me and that I am completely free to make of it what I will then the non-duality of subject and object will remain unknown to me. Devotion to the pure and true is a way of connecting beyond the realm of duality. If we pray *lama khyenno*, "Guru, think of me, hold me in your mind," what we are saying is, "I can't do it by myself. I need help". With this we start to really take refuge because we are alive to the fact that we need refuge. We are lost, adrift on the ocean of samsara. Help is available, always. Yet only the open heart of devotion can find the true deep helper.

Dependent origination points out that on the basis of this that arises. On the basis of seeing myself as an autonomous ego-self, I look at you as other. Therefore I need to put myself first and so I will try to get from this environment what I like and avoid what I don't like. Taking myself to be an independent agent I have to manage the continuity and happiness of myself by constantly adjusting my relation with the environment. This ceaseless self-referential activity is what we call karma. It is the basis of developing tendencies which will manifest as future forms of limitation. However, devotion to the unreifiable actuality of the ever-present enlightened ones gradually allows us to trust them rather than our imagined self. Devotion brings you close to the openness of relaxed awareness. I need you! We pray as if we are in a small boat that has been caught by a strong current. I'm being washed out to sea, but if I can throw a rope and tie it around the buoy floating in the water I can stabilise my little boat of self that is carried this way and that by whatever is arising in my mind, by all my hopes and fears and so on. If I tie my rope onto a thought, it is not going to keep me safe because thoughts are always on the move. Even people who are good and kind are not very secure either. They can get sick, have mental health problems, become unemployed; all kinds of events can shift how they are and how available they are for us. Devotion is a way of linking our ever-shifting self-patterns to what is actually stable. This means the apparitional forms of emptiness. The only secure unchanging refuge is emptiness itself, for it is the site of the self-releasing of all forms of limitation.

OUR MIND: STILLNESS AND MOVEMENT

The mind has two aspects: stillness and movement. The forms of the world including ourselves, our families, our friends, our dogs are all movement. Whatever manifests in whatever way will change and vanish. It does not remain as it is. This is not a specific problem linked to qualities of this particular arising. It is not that if we could just try harder, we would be able to stabilise manifestation. Everything is moving. The future is unknown.

17

You cannot secure the moving. It is not as if some 'thing' is moving – the moving is the arising and vanishing of appearance. The moving is always moving and will not be stilled. Yet you can find stillness – but not in the moving. You can settle into the unchanging, and this is what we explore when we examine the emptiness of all phenomena. The movement of phenomena is inseparable from their unchanging emptiness. Thus all movement is unborn. The word emptiness is not very beautiful in English. It indicates a kind of absence, that something is missing. However it also points to possibility, to potential, to availability for appearance.

At this moment I have tea in my cup, and so the potential of the cup is limited by the presence of the tea. If I were to add some coffee to the tea it wouldn't taste very good, so at this time the tea seems to be the limit of the cup. The cup itself is not limited, but situationally its function becomes limited by the presence of a specific content. When I finish drinking the tea, I return the cup to its potential. It is no longer a cup of tea. It is just a cup. So this is the same with us. When we sit in the practice and we open to our open empty mind, we find that it is free of fixed personal content as all our thoughts, feelings, sensations arise and pass. The cup itself is a receptive space; it is always empty even when filled since it is not contaminated by its transient content. In this regard, the open empty cup is like the sky, always empty. Thus the cup is filled without being filled, just as when the sky is full of clouds, it is filled with cloud and yet it is not filled, because the sky remains open and empty and when the wind blows the clouds away, the sky is revealed just as it has always been, fresh, ready and available.

This example illuminates the open potential of the mind. In fact it is not like a cup which is always filled with something else. It is more like a mirror which is filled with its own reflections. This creative potential of both mind and mirror are evoked by circumstances. Due to this, that arises. When the mind is relaxed and open many different experiences arise and pass without leaving a trace. Images like cup and mirror illuminate certain aspects of the mind. Yet it is vital to experience that the mind is not a thing. It is infinitely empty and free of any sense of container and contained.

However when not relaxed and open the mind can appear as a thing which has both stable and varying content. For the ego-self the mind is like a cup, held within the bigger permanent cup of the self. When a thought or memory arises in my mind, it is as if this containing cup is a paper cup and the thought starts to be absorbed into the texture of the cup and remain there as a memory trace. Then I, the cup, feel sad or happy that that happened. It seems to remain with me evoking further thoughts and feelings. The container, I, me, myself, seems to fuse with the transient content and so I'm sad, just sad. Then another thought comes giving me the feeling that I do not want to be sad. Then another thought indicates that I need to do something to stop being sad. The effort to get me free of sad thoughts immerses me in other thoughts. If we are attentive to what is occurring we painfully come to see that no amount of involved manipulation will bring us freedom from involvement. Involvement feeds more involvement. The truth is, our ego-self is empty of its own content. If we could see this, we would gain a relative freedom, the freedom to see that I am a cup, and so I can be a cup of orange juice or coffee or whisky or whatever. Yet the quality of our ego-self is an on-going anxiety that seeks to find our reliable enduring self – grasping onto the idea of self as if it could be made substantial by belief.

It is this delusion that hides the actual ever-open sky-like nature of the mind. If I am determined to secure my finite identity how will I be open to seeing that I am not other than this infinite openness. Spurning the ever-open, I turn towards the false and misleading security of my definition of myself as being like this. Believing that I am knowable, and on the basis of knowing myself to be like this, it is clear that I am not like that and I can't do that. I wouldn't be me if I did that. The ego-self has a very small portfolio of possibilities. The open potential of awareness which can manifest in many different forms is grounded in awareness being inseparable from emptiness. However, the ego exists on the basis of being some-thing. Again and again it insists 'I am this', and in this way it continues ignoring its own open ground. This is a terrible paradox for in order to maintain myself I have to limit and mutilate my potential, but if I was to relax and open, I wouldn't be me. This tension is usually managed by being forgetful of our potential and focusing on self-maintenance.

We spend time looking at the buddhist view and understanding in order to be able to sing a sweet dharma lullaby. We sing, "Sweet little ego, you go to sleep. I'm going to meditate so sleep beside me." Then, through being present in the meditation and not getting involved in what is arising, our consciousness, which always takes an object is gradually released from this habitual obligation, so that its true nature can be revealed.

The term consciousness refers to the clarity of the mind when it is mediated through the veil of duality. Instead of open empty knowing, fresh each moment, we have a sense that I know this and I know that and I can build up a vast edifice of knowing. The pure knowing, which is the presence of awareness, is self-liberating, always open, always available. Whereas consciousness is ceaselessly filling itself with stored events, images, ideas, memories, plans and so on. To be conscious of some-thing is to engage in the construction of the thing you are conscious of.

Conceptual clarity is artificial and much duller than intrinsic clarity. The former is produced by effort while the latter is effortless, like the illumination offered by the rising sun. Our reliance on concepts seems illuminating within the dualistic frame of 'I know something', yet it is actually dulling since it cannot reveal the true source of knowing which is does not rely on concepts. This is why in the practice we do not interfere with the free flow of experience. We are present without being reliant on anything – and this way we come to trust unborn ungraspable awareness.

Emptiness doesn't mean empty of everything. It means empty of things. Consciousness employs concepts to construct the illusory things that we seem to encounter whereas primordial knowing sees directly that there are no things, that we are living in a world of light. So, when we sit, calm and open, spacious like the sky suffused with illuminating presence, appearances arise and shift and change like sunlight glinting on the tops of the waves, on and on and on ... Within this clarity there is participation as illusory forms including our own body and everything we see. In order to find ourselves as this light, radiant vitality of openness, we have to let go of our addiction to holding on to heavy darkness, the mental obscuration of believing in substantial things.

The intrinsic is ever present. It is not hidden yet it is revealed when we desist from veiling it. We veil it with our constructs, with what is gathered together or made on the basis of the dualistic thoughts of sentient beings. Unawareness, ignorance, is the dullness of not opening to the intrinsic. After the initial sudden experience of something, instead of relaxing back into the intrinsic with that moment as part of it, it is turned into something else by grasping, by holding on to it as special. This is the initiatory moment, the beginning of samsara, the concealing of the open with imaginings of the real. The real is always imagined and the certitude of belief in this imagining seems more attractive to the nascent ego-self than the ungraspable quality of illusion. This imagining of the real, the existent, is a friend of the ego because it obscures the openness which is the site of awareness. Unable to access direct non-dual knowing the ego imagines all kinds of interpretations, theories, philosophies and so on.

When Siddhartha sits under the bodhi tree and decides that he is not going to search anymore for something else, that he is not going to move until all is clear, he gives up trying. He doesn't move his body, voice or mind despite the provocations of the mara demons. His habitual tendencies and impulses lose their power and his mind remains settled and relaxed. With this he becomes buddha; all limitations cleared away and all good qualities manifest.

He did not clear the obstacles away. By not confirming the obstacles as a necessary part of yourself they vanish by themselves. There is then space for clarity illuminating the true qualities of everything encountered. The Buddha's awakening or enlightenment is not the reward for effort. Rather by not indulging habit formations and deluded interpretations there is no basis for limitation. All limiting and limited experiences of self, other, entities, and all that seems to exist arise due to the energy of self-protective dualistic consciousness. When that perverse energy of reification and selection is not activated by belief in delusion then they fade away. Their power was our belief in them. With the vanishing of the obscurations and constructed habit-formations enlightenment shines forth. Although, in the buddhist literature we can find many teachings employing the metaphor of a journey and the need to make effort, if buddha nature was a construct, it would be impermanent. All compounded things are impermanent. Only the intrinsic, the unborn, is uncompounded and so not subject to decay and oblivion. Therefore we should focus on the intrinsic. This is the message of the first statement of Garab Dorje: see your original face, open to your unborn essence.

Awareness of the unborn is the key to awakening from the deluded dreams of reification. Awareness is the illuminating vitality of the mind. It shows how it is without creating anything. The light of illumination is already burning. Now, if there is a light shining and I turn my back towards the light, what I see in front of me is my shadow. That shadow is samsara. If we turn around, if we turn our attention away from all the entities we imagine, and turn towards the light, we find that we are translucent, the light is shining through us. We are already light, light refracted into many colours, many patterns. We have no substantial essence or fixed identity – these are mere concepts we adhere to. Our heaviness, our dullness, our limitations all arise from ignoring the unlimited light of which we are a part. By reifying appearances into entities each with their own existence we diminish our access to the openness we inhabit. In meditation it is important not to try too hard. We are not trying to get somewhere or to get rid of something. Enlightenment is not something that you can get or make or buy. We can relax into it because it is already here.

In the dzogchen tradition there are so many terms indicating 'from the very beginning', 'primordial', 'unchanging' and so on. These terms are referring to the intrinsic completion of all that occurs. Every appearance, every experience is within the unborn mind and is inseparable from emptiness. They are not tainted by duration or location and so are fresh, being freshly present in the primal moment which is always now. If we open to this then we see there is nothing for us to achieve and how we are is simply how we are – a momentary patterning of the unborn. As with a reflection in a mirror there is the possibility of ungraspable appearance or of grasping at interpretations of the reified image. The less we do the more we will see with fresh eyes unconditioned by our habit-formations. Involvement in what is occurring with a bias directing our saying 'yes' to this and 'no' to that, shows that we are still within the paradigm of duality, oscillating between being subject or object.

MOTHER OF WISDOM

We can now approach emptiness from a different angle which may help us find our own way of opening to the fact that we are manifestly present here and yet cannot be defined by concepts such as existent or non-existent.

We will look at the verse *Salutation to the Mother of Wisdom* which belongs to the class of literature called the *Prajna Paramita* or transcending discerning wisdom. The wisdom which transcends duality and discerns the true nature of experience is the wisdom of emptiness. This is written about elaborately and less elaborately. Our verse here is only four lines and very precise. Its meaning can be further essentialised in the mantra: *TADYATA GATE GATE PARAGATE PARASAMGATE BODHI SOHA* which means "It is like this, it is gone, gone, gone beyond, gone fully beyond, awakened, so it is." Moreover it

is also fully contained in the syllable A (ཨ) which is the symbol of emptiness.

SALUTATION TO THE MOTHER OF WISDOM

སྨྲ་བསམ་བརྗོད་མེད་ཤེས་རབ་ཕ་རོལ་ཕྱིན།

MA	SAM	JOE	ME	SHE RAB	PHA ROL	CHIN
speech	thought	expression	without	wise discerning, (transcendent, beyond dualism)	far side	gone

Transcendental wise discerning beyond speech, thought or expression

མ་སྐྱེས་མི་འགགས་ནམ་མཁའི་ངོ་བོ་ཉིད།

MA	KYE	MI	GAG	NAM KHAI	NGO WO	NYI
not	born	not	stopping	sky's	true essence	itself

Is unborn and unceasing like the essence of the sky.

སོ་སོ་རང་རིག་ཡེ་ཤེས་སྤྱོད་ཡུལ་བ།

SO	SO	RANG RIG	YE SHE	CHOE	YUL WA
each	thing	intrinsic awareness	original knowing	activity	arena

This is the arena of activity of original knowing, intrinsic awareness revealing each appearance just as it is.

དུས་གསུམ་རྒྱལ་བའི་ཡུམ་ལ་ཕྱག་འཚལ་ལོ༔

DUE	SUM	GYAL WAI	YUM	LA	CHAG TSHAL LO
times	three	victors', buddhas'	Mother#	to	salutation

(past, present, future)

there is no buddhahood without awakening to emptiness

We bow to and praise the Mother of all the Buddhas of the three times.

Transcendental supreme knowing beyond speech, thought or expression, unborn and unstopped, in essence like the sky, the arena of original knowing illuminating whatever occurs: we salute the mother of all the buddhas of the three times.

"Transcendent supreme knowing or intuition is beyond speech, thought or expression," and yet, of course, in buddhism there are many, many words. The teachings are a form of compassion. Wisdom cannot be articulated: how it is, is how it is. This has to be directly encountered. As soon as you apply concepts to it, you're talking about it, and this acts to turn it into an object, into a thing that can be known and discussed. But when you see clearly – there is nothing to say. The buddha taught in order to help other people. He didn't do it for himself. He knew that he couldn't directly give the people what he had experienced. They would each have to open to the truth of their own mind in order for the truth to shine forth. It is not a good idea to talk about our meditation experience with other people apart from our teachers. Talking about it turns it into something, and as soon as you formulate something you enter the possibility of comparing and contrasting: my meditation today is not as good as it was yesterday. Such conceptualization can only make meditation more difficult. We are not trying to progress anywhere. We are easing ourselves into just being here. You can't make yourself just be here. You have to relax into being here. The here and now is always already here and now and is not to be found elsewhere. Although in the tradition we talk of yanas, which means vehicles, we are not going anywhere so we don't need brakes or an accelerator. There is nothing to stop and nothing to encourage. If I am not simply here, my mind will take me somewhere else. So, release identification with the constructs embedded in speech, thought and expression.

Transcendent supreme knowing is the wisdom of emptiness which takes us across to the far side, from samsara to nirvana, from duality to non-duality. We want to cross to the far side of the river. On this side we have the pseudo-stability of our habitual sense of self. The river is this ceaseless flow of possibilities, the river of mental content, thoughts, memories, plans, hopes, desires and all the many things which can flow through us as the stream, the santana of our experience. When we reify them we are overwhelmed and retreat back to the seeming safety of the known. By not being caught by thoughts and other occurrences we see the emptiness of these occurrences and so are freed from their grasp. Now from openness we can participate without reification, projection of value or attachment. With this we are on the other side yet not conditioned by the stream.

Supreme knowing or discerning wisdom is indicated by the term *sherab* in Tibetan. *She* means knowing and *rab* means best. The best knowing is the non-conceptual knowing of emptiness. This knowing is direct, undeniable and yet inexpressible. In our tradition the example is given of someone who does not know what the term 'sweet' is. You can use many words to explain but they still don't get it. So then you put a little honey on their tongue – Oh! So this is 'sweet'. They have direct experience, a true knowing, but they also cannot say how it is, only what it is like.

Transcendent knowing means not to engage in the unnecessary activity of building up pictures of the things we reify. You are standing on this shore, you don't enter into the river, you never enter the river, yet you are not hiding from the flow. It is as if it flows through you without touching you. When you are simply here, at rest, open, free of lack and excess then the idea of this shore and that shore doesn't arise. If you were on the other shore, you would be … here. Where can you be in life? It is always here. It is always now. Thus transcendent or intuitive or incisive knowing reveals to you that you are already here. Here is where we are. What is this like, this here? I can say I'm sitting on a chair which is a little bit hard, but now I'm not here now I'm talking about the chair, I'm here looking at this laptop in front of me, which is on a table with some yellow plastic on top of it. If I try to tell you about what is here, I go there. 'There' is concept-based while 'here' is direct and free from commentary. Here is inexpressible and ungraspable. Here is silent.

The ultimate contraction of all THE HEART SUTRA literature is just the sound of 'A'. 'A' is the presence of emptiness. It is a sound – 'A'– a slight aspiration of the flow of our breath. It has no content; it is the basis of the many elaborations of language: mama, papa and so on. 'A' is the most simple, unelaborated sound, it is just the silent breath, turned up slightly on a dimmer switch. Based on 'A' we have all the words that support all the concepts that fabricate the experience of samsara, of being on this shore. 'A' is the basis of these illusory imaginings and 'A' is the presence of emptiness. Every phenomenon, every experience, every constituent of ourselves and our world is inseparable from emptiness. Emptiness is their foundation, their basis, their mother – and they remain, in their actuality, non-dual with her. Every-thing is empty of self, empty of inherent existence and in the light of this it becomes obvious that to make progress is simply to be here. This deconstructs our assumption of progress: we progress to being here by not going anywhere else.

Now, if you step into the river, without knowing how it is, it will carry you somewhere. The person who steps in the river is a 'someone' stepping into 'some-thing' – and so these two reified entities act on each other. When we directly see that we are not a someone, that we are an illusory pattern inseparable from the field of illusory patterns then the illusory river can no longer carry us away. This is our meditation: we sit, relax and open. Yet we can still find that we are floating down the river. Some thought, memory or emotion arises and we merge with it and are carried by it. It seems to be taking us somewhere else. Where should we be? If you were doing basic shamatha practice of calming the mind and you were focusing on the sensation at your nostrils, when you found your mind wandering, you would bring it back to the nostrils. I should be here. I've gone there. I better get back!

However in our practice, we sit and sometimes suddenly find ourselves off somewhere else. But is there anywhere else to go? So, in that moment we don't do anything. We do not mobilise dualistic consciousness and think about what to do. Relaxing into the state of 'A' we find ourselves in unborn awareness. As soon as you are aware, you are here. Stay with the hereness of here. There is nowhere better to be than here. Even that is not a very helpful formulation, because it is still in terms of hierarchy of place. In fact there is only ever here and now. When you are present in awareness, the river keeps flowing. Yet now the river is a flow of empty illusory forms. They are empty, they lack existence and so there is nothing to gain or lose, nothing to adopt or reject. Awareness is still and unmoving. The creative potential of the mind is always moving. This creativity creates patterns, the patterns of our experience – but it cannot create real, existent, entities. They are delusions however much we, as ego-self, believe in them.

At first, when we start to practise, we make a division between stillness and movement. We think my mind is always moving, I need to make it become still. But the calm which you create by practising shamatha is artificial, because it is a construct. You build it up, and then, if you don't do the practice for a while, you lose the capacity. This verse, the essence of THE HEART SUTRA, shows us that the stillness of the mind discerns movement clearly without being caught up in it. Wisdom illuminates what is there without being carried away. The one that is carried away is dualistic consciousness. Consciousness needs an object but the clear discernment of transcendent wisdom doesn't need an object. In this explanation I am using both the terminology of the mahayana transcendent wisdom texts and the texts of dzogchen. I am doing this to illuminate our practice. When looking at the views and their implicit assumptions we can notice differences of axiom and implication. But for busy people who want to awaken to how their mind actually is and gain liberation from confusion such differences are not so important. We need to study our own mind, our actual vibrant experience and find ourselves in the here and now.

When we are present with whatever is occurring, clarity is immediate and inexpressible. This clarity is unimpeded because it is without prejudice, judgement, reification or selectivity. It shows directly that all that occurs is equal and even in its unborn emptiness. No occurrence is superior or inferior to any other. Nothing is special and yet this wisdom is transcendent and so, from within the shadowland of samsara, it is special. It is amazing; it takes you where you want to go, right to the heart of emptiness—where you have been from the very beginning. We have to remember that this verse is a dualistic expression of the non-dual. It is like a parent talking to a child: they explain to the child within the frame of reference that the child is operating in. But actually, according to our dzogchen view, we're not going anywhere else. If you want to go somewhere, you are going to be wandering around in samsara. Everybody is wandering here, there and everywhere. The actual is inexplicable.

If the ego were to taste even a moment of this it would feel quite lonely. The ego lives in a dialogue – with itself or with others. It is co-emergent. It believes that it can share experiences with others. But you can't share your experience. All that you can share is words 'about' what you think you experienced. The narrative can only come after the event. The event itself is not a concept and cannot be caught or described by a concept. You can phone a friend and say, "Hey, I just went to an amazing new restaurant, the food is wonderful." The food is described as something existent; you can perceive qualities in the food. This is the domain of language. In talking about something we feel connected, we are sharing our experience. However this is only true within the paradigm of delusion where we encounter real, existing entities. There is nothing to say about the actual, about the fact that all experience is inseparable from emptiness. But the ego wants to say something! Because if I share something with you, I am confirmed as the one who speaks. The ego weaves its existence through thinking and talking.

We like to have friends because our friends confirm the validity of our being who we take ourselves to be. But from the point of view of dharma we are not who we think we are. The ego is concerned with narrative, with the construction of accounts of how I am, how you are and so on. But this clear discerning wisdom, this acuity, this sharpness of the mind, sees the lack of substance in whatever is being talked about. We think and talk entities into existence. All entities, all isolates, all existents are products of our illusion generated by our own mental activity. They have no inherent existence. They do not stand alone. Subject and object are born together as delusion while remaining unborn. If I say, for example, that I want to tell you about my friend Ben, I am going to tell you about a person who is not here. Yet as soon as I start to tell you about Ben, I am making Ben for you. If there is another Ben somewhere else, the 'real' Ben, that's not our Ben; our Ben is the one I am preparing with you. When we say something about Ben you have to make sense of what I said. You interpret my words according to your own association. In this way we are both creating or cooking up Ben. We call this dish Ben as if we are talking about the same person. Yet we taste or experience Ben according to our own palate. Only conventionally, only in terms of words do we share an idea and experience of Ben. Here we see the nature of ignorance. As we ignore the actual, the 'as is', we start to imagine how it is, the 'as if'.

If I say Ben lives in Paris, I am asserting that there is a Paris, and in that Paris there is a Ben. These are ideas. The thoughts that I have about Ben when I start to talk about him have nothing to do with Ben as a living ever-changing stream of phenomena. As soon as I take my thoughts and words to have a real existent referent, I am confident that my words are in touch with and express something true about this referent. If you do the same then we have confidence that when we are talking about Ben we are not inventing him but are honestly engaging with our sense of how he is. You might wonder why James is talking about Ben. So now you can think about something (his talking) which is already a description of something (Ben). Talking takes you away from the actual, while generating the illusion that it is connecting you with the actual. This is why you cannot think or talk your way out of samsara. If you fall into language and believe that it connects you to the real then you don't see it as a self-liberating emergence in the moment. Now the illusory seems real and confusion reigns.

This is the play of mental activity. This is the creativity of the mind. We can create stories about Ben, stories about presidents, stories about great lamas and so on. There is no actual person to be found. You are inventing them by your speaking of them. By believing your own words you are stupefying yourself. You are thickening your reliance on dualistic consciousness further obscuring your access to intrinsic awareness. By taking the imagined to be real you make it more difficult to see how your mind is. Our mind is open, empty, clear and luminescent, manifesting unborn patterns of connectivity. It is not a thing.

If you look in politics, economics, education, everywhere you see the reification of the imagined. It is this that hides the truth of the mind. We are actually talking about experience, not about real entities. Without the mind there is no experience. We're not talking about real people – there are no real people. The word real indicates a thing, an entity. Yet when we look clearly, without imagining, projecting or interpreting we see that no entities can be found. This is a relative or analysis-based experience of transcendent wisdom. Then we need to deepen this beyond the intellect so that it arises as the intrinsic clarity of the ground source. This clarity shows the actual luminosity or transparency of all that had previously seemed solid, definite and real. By awakening to the intrinsic purity of samsara the opaque becomes bright. No outer forms of your life need to be changed because now it is clear that they are dream-like and devoid of true existence. Everything, including all aspects of what you take to be yourself, are non-dual with the ever-open ground; emptiness, the mother of all. Then you have no position to defend since no-thing is established and all thoughts and feelings are without referent. This frees us from the eight worldly concerns: hope for pleasure and fear of pain; hope for gain and fear of loss; hope for praise and fear of blame; hope for good reputation and fear of bad reputation. All arisings are ungraspable. All beings are beyond our definition of them. So instead of trying to control others or fit them into our template we can release them (and ourselves) from our ideas about them and open to how they manifest. With this we can have true contact and appreciation without appropriation.

With transcendent wisdom we see everything is the play of emptiness; it is illusion, like a rainbow in the sky, like a mirage, like the reflection of the full moon in a pond. When you look at the moon in the pond it seems obvious that something is there, but this depends on your positioning. If you see the reflection of the moon in a pond and you step back, even a few metres, you don't see the moon anymore. The reflection arises from the relation between where the moon is, how its light hits the pond, and where you are standing. It is relative. The showing of the moon depends on these causes and conditions, as does a mirage or a rainbow.

We see something yet it does not exist in itself. You see your mother but she doesn't exist in herself. All you can ever see is your mother, you don't see your siblings' mother, and you don't see her according to the eyes of her friends. This is because you are creating your mother. Her manifestation is a potential for interpretation. Everything in the world arises as the interplay between the potential of the object-side and the potential of the subject-side. It is how we see it. If you go into a drawing studio with a live model, the people doing the drawings come up with very different interpretations. They draw according to what they see mediated through their templates of interpretation. We walk, talk, eat, sleep and interpret these experiences according to our pre-existing patternings. We can only experience the world according to us because there is no real self-arising world 'out there'. The seeming similarities in the way we can talk about our experiences is due to the similarities of our karmic habits which give rise to our human birth in our specific cultures. Each of us is a repertoire of patternings of participation. We are not a fixed thing, a person who does this or a person who does that. We are not a singular maker or doer. Rather we are part of the revelation of the field which displays itself as the interplay of emergent subject-side and object-side. We participate with the field as part of the field – sometimes seemingly as productive agent, sometimes seemingly as reactive recipient. The terms 'subject' and 'object' do not refer to real fixed entities but to ever-shifting sites of emergence in the field. They are co-evoking, co-emergent and are non-dual. If we relax out of the egoic need to define and control then we can start to enjoy the freedom of playful co-emergent participation. We are neither master nor slave – we participate according to circumstances.

This world is revealed to me, and this is my world. This does not mean that the world is my own private fantasy. This is not an idealistic position. Rather, the world reveals itself according to how I participate. Clear seeing, discerning, insightful seeing is the mode of participation which gives us access to the mother of all the buddhas. This is incomprehensible through the medium of concepts. We need to open to our own intrinsic unborn awareness and the clarity will manifest.

On a relative level it can help to watch how other people live and see that they do things you don't do. If you go to other people, look at how they design their homes. Wild! How is this possible? How could they want to live like this? That is because it is their world. It rings true for them. We are a range of vibrations. Everything in the world is vibration. We make decisions according to our resonances with what we encounter in the world. Somebody wears a very bright orange sweater, we look at it – 'Oh, that's too much!' But not for the person who is wearing it. Their vibration and the orange are quite in harmony, but for us it is disturbing. This is the play of emptiness – beyond judgement, beyond right and wrong. If you make a judgement, it is just another movement in the playful creation of this empty luminous patterning – nothing is established, nothing is real.

For meditators this first line of the verse is saying: the truth is silent, but you don't have to shut up. Because when you move, when you communicate, this is the movement of the energy of the ground, revealed by the clarity of unsayable ground. You can live truthfully but you can't speak the truth. The function of speech is not to reveal wisdom but to offer non-dual ethical connectivity. When we speak, we are participating with others in the co-emergence of patterns of illusion, of ungraspable immediate connectivity. If you stay with what is manifesting, being present with the emergent brings the next moment of emergence. The river never stops flowing. You're on the bank and in the river at the same time. There's no contradiction between them. As THE HEART SUTRA says, *"Form is not different from emptiness, emptiness is not different from form."* The river is not different from the bank; the flowing, the moving, is not different from the still. The still is not something at all, and the flow is not made up of a series of entities. This inexpressible luminosity is uninterrupted and unceasing.

When the teaching of transcendent knowing was first given on the Vulture Peak Mountain in Rajgir in Bihar, India, there were many people present who fell unconscious. This occurred because what the buddha was pointing towards is not something you can put into your existing frame of reference. This is like pouring boiling water into a paper bag. The ordinary concepts that we have for managing our life in samsara cannot entertain emptiness. Emptiness is not just another concept, a better concept or a buddhist concept. It is the de-reification of all concepts and when you dissolve the basis for this reification or solidification you are in play-time.

The second line of the verse, **"unborn and unstopped, in essence like the sky."** This is referring to the transcendent knowing pointed to in the first line. This inexpressible clarity of the mind is unborn. This means it hasn't become a thing. It is not to be found anywhere. To be born is to come out of the mother; to separate and have the umbilical cord cut so that the baby is on its own. Of course babies need a lot of care but now the baby is considered to be an entity. However, the mind of the buddha is not an entity, it is not like anything that we know. It is not an entity and it is beyond comparing and contrasting. Yet it is not nothing at all because it is unstopped, unimpeded. The flow of experience continues but now experience is unreified and ungraspable. It just is – immediate … vanishing. Ordinarily experience is mediated through the dualistic notion of the knower and the known. Thus, if I look at my watch, I know that this is my watch. My watch is the thing that I know, but I am not my watch; the knower and the known seem to be very different. However, this first word, 'unborn', indicates the luminous awareness of the mind. When this is clear, what arises is unstoppable illusory experience. Illuminated by awareness, this experience is not something apart from the mind. It is neither exactly the same nor different, just as the reflection in the mirror is neither separate from the mirror nor exactly the same. Unborn awareness is inseparable from the ceaseless display of ever-changing experience.

Then the line says that in essence it is like the sky. You can't catch the sky. It is unborn, without centre or edge. It is not a thing that you can find. You never find 'the' sky, just this sky, this sky as it is at this moment. On a clear day it looks blue, the wind blows through it, perhaps carrying the scent of mimosa or some fragrance. At other times many different kinds of clouds move in the sky. We see them in the sky, we can't take the cloud out of the sky. The sky and the cloud are not two and not one, they are non-dual just as in THE HEART SUTRA "Form is emptiness, emptiness is form." They are not merged as one, but neither are they two. Although emptiness pervades all appearance and is beyond thought, it can help to consider the empty aspect *(sTong-Cha)* and an appearance aspect *(sNang-Cha)*. From this point of view they are like two sides of the same coin – always together and yet not identical.

Our mind is empty and full at the same time. The fact that it is full doesn't block its emptiness. It can only be full because it is empty; if it had something in of itself, it couldn't be filled. It would have a half-openness or a quarter-availability. The mind is like the sky, inherently empty, so there is no limit to availability. When the mind is full it is full of empty appearance. Thus it is empty even while it is full. Moreover the appearances that fill the mind arise for us as experience and are self-arising and self-liberating. This is their actual quality although within the frame of duality this is hidden by reification, grasping and projection and by our divisive selective tendency of adopting and rejecting.

Our life is inseparable from our circumstances and although we might like to draw a circle around ourselves and stay safe inside, we are not able to function if we do that. For example, in Tibet, if people did a long solitary retreat, they would put mantras and signs outside the cave where they were living. People generally respected this and so did not intrude. But when the Chinese army arrived the symbols offered no protection.

This brings us to the third line: **"the arena of original knowing illuminating whatever occurs."** This is the vast hospitality of the sky-like mind which allows the flow of experience, so that the precise details of whatever is occurring are clearly seen. This is the arena or playground of transcendent primordial knowing, knowing which has been present yet ignored from the very beginning. This intrinsic unconstructed unartificial is not cognitive and cumulative. It is immediate and intuitive. If I look out of my window just now, I see some people on the road and the way the cars are parked and so on.

Then something catches my eye. So, I look a bit more, 'Oh, what is that? That is unusual!' Now, in that moment of examining one thing through the medium of dualistic consciousness everything else vanishes, and thus my specific interest becomes a violence against the equal value of all that is occurring. Without even being conscious of doing it I am making this more important than that. This third line is pointing to a very different way of knowing, a relaxed open panoramic vision allowing each detail to arise with full value. It is not either/or. It is not either everything or just this one thing. It is the precise detail of the whole revealed all at once without selection or effort.

With the clarity of transcendent knowing we are not trying to work out what is there. We are not trying to make sense of what is going on. The world is not a problem for us to solve. We are receiving the gift of all that is arising here and now. Arising and passing, this moment of our experience is in itself all there is, and yet the flow of experience does not stop. It is ceaseless. Like the waves in the ocean there is another wave and another wave and another wave. There is no clear boundary between the waves, and yet each wave is its own precise self. That is why our key meditation practice of Guru Yoga enables us to relax, release fixation, and be present with whatever is occurring. However, if we get overly connected with the details of an aspect of the field, the danger is not just that we increase our attention to that particular detail, but that this attention quickly invites the projection of value. If something caught my eye, there must be a reason, so I should look again, 'Ah, this interests me!' That doesn't sound very dangerous, yet I am losing openness to the whole. Something catches my attention, I mentally catch hold of it, and now it has caught me and I am caught up in it.

Awareness doesn't take an object. It doesn't need an object. The mirror doesn't need to have anything reflected in it. At night-time when you put the light off, it doesn't become less of a mirror because it is not showing any reflection. But if you were to stretch a canvas on a frame and hang it on the wall, every time you see it it is saying, don't you want to paint? I'm not finished yet, I'm a little bit naked to be hanging on the wall, give me some clothes. There is a kind of demand. Something needs to be done.

It is just like this in the meditation practice: you are sitting, appearance is coming and going. I am needy. I want something. I don't even know what I want. Perhaps it is this, perhaps it is not. And in that state we are very easily distracted, following different kinds of experience. This is a sign that we are moving in the bandwidth of consciousness. We have not settled into awareness, and in that sense this is a sign that we are still alienated from our mother. Emptiness is not enough for us. We want something to hold on to, and so ignoring the openness of emptiness we imagine something we can get hold of.

The beginning of the first line of this verse states that transcendent wisdom can't be spoken, can't be thought – there is no way to express it in any way. Yet consciousness insists that it can define wisdom in such a way that it can be accessed by thinking about it. This generates many views but none of them are the direct actuality. Yet because we are so used to relying on concepts, it is as if the concept can stand in for the actual. This is self-deception. Dualistic consciousness is what we have relied on for a very long time; it is easy to turn to as the one who can make any situation clear. It does this by re-patterning the concepts we are familiar with so that it is as if we have gained a new and useful insight. But no matter how hard you try you cannot think your way out of samsara. Concepts are in servitude to the delusional ego and like the ego they turn their back on their own mother. However if we release ourselves from our reliance on concepts and simply relax and stay open, we find that everything is already clear. What is it? It is the display of emptiness. This is how emptiness shows itself. The reflection is how the mirror shows itself. The reflection isn't the same as the mirror, but the ungraspable reflection is how you know it is a mirror.

Awareness or intrinsic knowing is non-selective; it shows everything all at once and very precisely. What we experience as subject and object are both illuminated by the light of awareness. Our experience is not other than the inter-play of the ungraspable vectors of the energy of awareness. Just as the sun gives both, light and heat, so awareness illuminates and also energises the patterning of illusory phenomena. The dynamism of the emergent empty shapes allows us to improvise in the immediacy of the moment. It is through direct sensory contact that we find how we can collaborate with whatever occurs. Although all the movements we have made are available as a repertoire of moves, if the contact is truly open it is fresh and not dependent on the past. There is no need to rehearse any specific gestures. Rather we need to release our habitual ways of engaging so that authentic co-emergence can occur. You don't know how to do it or what to do, but like the mirror, if you are available, not already preoccupied, then you find illusory movement arising from openness and moving within openness. Co-emergence is not based on a conscious intention, it is the spontaneity of contact. If a thought arises such as "Oh, that was clumsy," and you go with that thought about the past, then you've lost co-emergence. But if the thought, "Oh, that was clumsy," is kept within the flow of experience it will influence the next movement without stopping the flow.

These three lines of the verse lead into the fourth and final one: **"We bow to and praise the Mother of all the Buddhas of the three times."** It is by opening to our own emptiness that we are able to see the truth of all phenomena. Our presence is non-dual with emptiness and the direct wisdom of this, the original knowing of non-duality, awakens us to being within the womb of the great mother, the transcendent wisdom of emptiness. This is where all buddhas are born. Born from emptiness, in emptiness, as the radiance of emptiness. This is the dharmakaya pure awareness from which and within which manifest the sambhogakaya clarity and the nirmanakaya responsivity. The quasi-autonomous ego-self has dissolved back into the flow of experience as its constituents break free of their wrapper of delusion.

Everything that arises is equal in emptiness as there is not one 'thing' that does not have this nature. There is no need to attribute value on the basis of liking and disliking since such discrimination does not arise in emptiness. No more adjusting, altering, making efforts to improve or discard what occurs. All appearances are intrinsically empty and are precisely and perfectly themselves as the radiance of emptiness.

In this life your mother showed you many things. This mother, the Great Mother is different. She doesn't show you 'things', she shows you the inseparability of appearances and emptiness. All that you take your self to be is appearance. You are the blossoming, the showing of emptiness. Therefore we open ourselves to our true mother and find how we actually are by opening within her infinite openness. When your unborn awareness awakens to this openness all remnant traces of reification vanish. You are ungraspable presence effortlessly manifesting apparitional patterns for the benefit of others.

The immediacy of presence frees you from reliance on accumulated knowledge and all experience is fresh in its co-emergence. 'I' as openness is unborn and 'I' as appearance is unstopped, ceaselessly manifesting. With this 'I' we awaken to the truth that I am the union of wisdom and kindness. With this, every possible appearance becomes inseparable from the truth of dharma and can be a means to attunement and liberating connectivity.

Anxiety is empty, depression is empty, psychosis is empty, happiness is empty, hopelessness is empty … emptiness is the one medicine that cures all problems. If you don't have emptiness as the basis of your life moment by moment, then you have solidification, reification, fragmentation and over-identification with parts so that the integrity of the whole remains unseen.

It is important not to grasp at trying to understand emptiness. It is not a thing, it is not an appearance. Simply sit, relax, open and avoid involvement in what occurs. Simply stay present with the one who doesn't understand emptiness. Don't fuse into this not knowing and don't stand apart from it. With this you see that the experience of dullness starts to change. It has actually been held in place by your own reification, so just sit.

The mind itself is like the sky, and the sky, as far as we know, doesn't get upset when it is full of grey clouds. It is just open. The ego is not just open, the ego has an agenda. So when we sit we relax and release our identification with the ego's agenda. We're not looking to what is arising to give us something. The sky doesn't have a lack; the mirror doesn't have a lack that the reflection might fill. Our awareness has no lack. But the ego-self is full of lack and hunger and need. The ego is patterning, ever-shifting patterning of energy formation moving in the open, empty sky of the mind. All beings have the potential to be buddha. Some have become buddha in the past, some are becoming buddha now, some will become buddha in the future, but they all have the same mother: emptiness. To meet our true mother we relax out of identificatory fixations and see that we are truly like the sky. Non-grasping is the door through which we must pass in order to become buddha. You have to be naked to pass through this door.

If you're sitting in the practice and trying to hold onto the mental habits that you have, your familiar emotions, your concerns with sensations in the body and so on, then you're burdened by this stuff, which is your stuff accumulated over lifetimes. However these fixations are not permanent. They are part of the repertoire out of which your current ego experiences are constellated. They are not intrinsic, nor truly definitive. Their arising is contingent, appearing due to shifting patterns of causes and conditions. There is no real connection between your unborn mind and what is arising, and yet this unborn mind is the sphere within which the ceaseless flow of experience is occurring.

The four lines of this verse show the basis for the practices of tantra and dzogchen. When we see that the ground or the openness, or the truth of how we are is empty of self-substance, the non-duality of emptiness and appearance becomes obvious. We are appearing in the field of arising experience, emerging in contact, changing all the time, breathing, stretching, scratching and so on. We are in ceaseless conversation with the environment and this is the ongoing revelation of the ceaseless energy of the mind itself.

What we call self and what we call environment arise together. Their co-emergence constitutes the undivided field of experience, the effortless arising instant presence of awareness and non-dual experience. In order to open to this I have to release myself from my fixation that 'this' is me, and find the open potential out of which this familiar formation of self and other arises without arising. The appearances constituting our experience are unborn and show us directly that self and other are also unborn. The non-duality or non-difference of appearance and emptiness is our true friend, the friend who dissolves all fixation. The ungraspable ground is exactly the ground from which everything arises. Everything is the smile of emptiness. All appearances are demonstrations of the availability of emptiness.

Emptiness is not a place somewhere far away. Emptiness is what is already here. A coin has two sides. You could say that these two sides are inseparable because they are always joined. But the side with the head on it and the other side are not the same. They are dual, not non-dual, because each side is different from the other. They are connected, joined, but they present as their difference. Emptiness is not like that.

Emptiness is not other than form. It is not form and emptiness, or even 'form which is empty'. If there is emptiness there is form. If there is form there is emptiness. Neither one nor two, neither the same nor different. They are an inseparable non-duality.

When you look into the truth of form you see that it is ungraspable and empty. If I look at my cup and I think about the cup, I make the cup more real. However if I start to take my thoughts out of the cup, my memory of where I got it, of how often I use it and so on, my opinions and judgements about the design, if I take myself out of the cup, the cup-ness of the cup is manifestly empty. Its seeming substance, its presence as some-thing, and its identity are all attributions that I make. I put the cup in the cup, and everything about it is made by the mind. This play of the mind itself has no substance, nothing is established. The cup is an aesthetic revelation. It is not an object out there that supports my cognitions. It is not an object but an undeniable and ungraspable presence. It will not support any definition or solid conclusion and yet in our blindness this does not stop us trying. Each moment of arising has an impact. We're touched and moved, and participate according to the circumstances. We are moving in the moving field, and yet our habits of reification can easily obscure this ungraspable freshness.

The freedom of the buddhas to be helpful for beings arises from their presence in the womb of the Great Mother. She is the mother in whom dissolve the relative truth qualities out of which we construct our familiar sense of self. We are then naked, and this naked openness has infinite potential to manifest in many different ways.

Our appreciation of emptiness often progresses from desisting from the imposition of the delusion of inherent existence. We come to see the falsity of the assertion that there are truly existing entities. Each appearance is the appearance of emptiness – it is not the appearance of 'something'. Each perceived 'something' is a mental event and remains unborn and unestablished within the vastness of the mind. Emptiness is pervasive, as the ever-fecund mother, the infinite mother full of potential. This is a plenum void, a void which is full, and there is no contradiction between full and empty. Infinite emptiness is not something that you can experience. We experience trees, pizzas and so on, but we don't experience emptiness because it is not an object of experience. However since all phenomena are inherently empty of self, when we experience any appearance we experience emptiness. If you see this directly you will be freed from the compulsion to construct.

Similarly, you can experience your consciousness. I can be conscious of the fact that I'm conscious that I need to do something at six o'clock this evening, because consciousness can seem to be the subject, yet it is also an object for a further consciousness. However awareness is not an experience, it is not an object. There is no experience of awareness. It is neither the experiencer nor the experience – yet it is also not other than these. Awareness is self-luminous, self-illuminating, offering nothing to grasp. The wisdom of emptiness is also called original knowing and awareness. The knowing they point to is not the knowing of this or that, but the self-luminous knowing of knowing, knowing as knowing. Clearly this evades language. Our dharma language is the finger pointing at the moon – it can't take you to the moon but it can help you to let go of all that keeps you from the moon.

Awakening to this mother who never abandons us is freedom itself. She is always available, very close, but not insistent. This bright mind, inseparable from emptiness, has no agenda; it is not trying to make you do anything. Emptiness is not trying to save anyone, because in emptiness there is no one to save. It is that simple. Awareness is peaceful and open and available. It has no door except the illusory doors fabricated by our own imaginings.

SALUTATION TO THE FATHER OF KINDNESS

ཧྲཱིཿ ཐུགས་རྗེ་ཆེན་པོས་འགྲོ་དྲུག་ཀུན་ལ་གཟིགསཿ

HRI	THU JE	CHEN POE	DRO	DRU	KUN	LA	ZIG
seed syllable	*compassion*	*great*	*travellers*	*six realms*	*all*	*to*	*look, see*

Hri. Looking with great kindness on all beings who wander in the six realms of samsara,

བྱམས་དང་སྙིང་རྗེས་སེམས་ཅན་ཀུན་ལ་སྙོམསཿ

JAM	DANG	NYING JE	SEM CHEN	KUN	LA	NYOM
love	*and*	*by kindness*	*sentient beings*	*all*	*to*	*hold in mind*

You hold all sentient beings in mind with your love and compassion.

དུས་གསུམ་བདེ་གཤེགས་མ་ལུས་སྐྱེད་པའི་ཡབཿ

DU	SUM	DE SHE		MA LU	KYE PAI	YAB
times	*three**	*sugatas, happily gone, buddhas*		*without exception*	*give rise to, develop*	*father*

*past, present, future

Father who gives rise to all the Buddhas of the three times,

འཕགས་པ་སྤྱན་རས་གཟིགས་ལ་ཕྱག་འཚལ་ལོཿ

PHA PA	CHEN RAE ZI	LA	CHA TSHAL LO
Arya, pure	*Avalokitesvara*	*to*	*bow*

Arya Chenrezi we bow to you!

Hri. Looking with great kindness on all beings who wander in the six realms of samsara, you hold all sentient beings in mind with your love and compassion. Father who gives rise to all the Buddhas of the three times, Arya Chenrezi we bow to you!

This verse is a homage to Avalokiteshvara (Tib. Chenrezi) as the father who ripens all beings into buddhahood by the skilful means of compassion. It begins with his seed syllable Hri. In the open space of dharmakaya awareness manifests five-coloured light which gathers together in the form of a letter Hri. This Hri then manifests Avalokiteshvara, the compassion of the sambhogakaya inseparable from the empty dharmakaya. The letter Hri is always present in the heart of Amitabha, the Buddha of the western direction. The name Amitabha indicates 'Infinite Light', the unimpeded illumination of the dharmakaya. To describe the process of manifestation of Avalokiteshvara in a different way, from the Hri in Amitabha's heart manifests a Hri which transforms into Avalokiteshvara.

All the buddhas and bodhisattvas except adibuddha Samantabhadra arise from their own specific intention. When Amitabha was a Bodhisattva he made a vow to save all beings by offering his name for them to rely on. He took it upon himself to become fully enlightened with much effort, so that beings, by just relying on his name, could take birth in his pure land of Sukhavati (*Tib. Dewachen*). Buddhas are not made in a standardised factory. Just as we have our own personalities and qualities, so do the bodhisattvas in the early stages of their careers. They each have a sense of how they might best benefit others. Avalokiteshvara made a vow to watch over all sentient beings and offer them his loving kindness so that they are never alone wherever they are. Thus the profoundest good intentions we have in our heart can ripen as an ethical presence that benefits all. The bodhisattva vow is inclusive – none must be left out and all must be welcomed. This in itself is a great method of dropping all the biased attitudes we have and all our tendencies to privilege some individuals and groups over others. The great and honourable heart that works for all is already latent within us. We awaken it by repeatedly dedicating all of the energy of our body, voice and mind in this in all our future lives, for the benefit of all. This means purifying all that limits beings and ripening their own buddha nature.

When we focus on a deity we want to experience their presence and we begin by saying Hri as this evokes the instant presence of Chenrezi, appearing within the open space of awareness where he abides. The first line reminds us that he is always **"looking with great kindness on all the beings who wander in the six realms of samsara."**

His kindness is inseparable from emptiness and so it is inexhaustible and instantly available everywhere. When we inhabit our ego-identity we have a limited area of operation since we are constrained by our self-interest and our self-definition. We are biased and therefore cannot see all clearly or respond to all evenly. How wonderful that Avalokiteshvara has freed himself from all limitation and obscuration. Looking on all beings equally, his loving kindness flows out to them, gently softening their hearts. This tender inclusion is free of judgement. He responds to the buddha nature which is equal in all beings. He is not evaluating their manifest qualities and judging some to be better than others. His love is not something we have to, or even could, earn. It is the freely available welcome of the enlightened mind. It is offered equally to those deemed to be good and those deemed to be bad. The virtuous are not offered more kindness than the bad as a reward. The bad are not offered more kindness as an antidote. Equal to all, for all are equal as they are.

In a world of self-concern and abandonment, knowing that we are being held in mind is a protection against nameless oblivion. Those in prison camps, those being tortured, the disappeared, all face not only the bleakness of their situation but also the loss of the warmth of inclusion. Avalokiteshvara's loving kindness is also available for them. When dictatorships become full of horror, one of the favourite pastimes of those in power is to make people disappear. They're walking on the street and suddenly a van drives up, they're grabbed and put inside and never seen again. They enter oblivion. The fact that some people remember them is important. The state wants them to be nothing at all, but we can remember. There are organisations like Amnesty International, which are very much concerned with remembering and making their names known. The very brave mothers of the disappeared in Argentina would be out every day protesting quietly in the square: we will not forget you! This is very important. Now we have more reporting on the conditions of the factory farming of animals. Thus many people with good hearts decide that they will not allow horror to be invisible. Avalokiteshvara is the embodiment of this concern – and in him it is ripened and enriched by being inseparable from emptiness. This ensures that his motive is always pure and not infected with the five poisons.

If we want to deeply connect with someone else, we look in their eyes. The name Avalokiteshvara means the seeing eye, the quick gaze that reveals how it is. If we look we will find that he is gazing at us; a warm gaze, like a mother to a baby. The mind itself is always alone, yet our manifestation is never alone. When we open to Avalokiteshvara we see that we can trust that we will never be abandoned. By connecting with the deity, through initiation, faith and practice, although we may forget the deity, the deity will never forget us.

Line 2 of the verse reminds us that he **"holds in mind all sentient beings with love and kindness."** If you take the bodhisattva vow, you promise to save all sentient beings. Then you go out for a walk in the town and you see how people spend their time, and then you start to cry. I promised to save people who don't want liberation, they want to get drunk. Ay, ay, ay, this is going to take a long time. Why didn't I look clearly at my limitations before I said these difficult words? But if we focus on our limitations then they would seem to be limitless and we would lose heart. The example of the great ones who have gone before gives us the courage to make this leap of faith and to offer to all beings this blank cheque: I will offer you whatever you need. This is an inconceivable generosity and it is only possible because the wisdom of emptiness, which is the light of our mind, is itself inconceivable. The inconceivable Mother shines forth as the inconceivable Father and their inseparable union lights the way.

In the mahayana tradition we say, *"For as long as it takes, in this and all my future lives, until all sentient beings are free, I will work for their benefit."* We are always already connected to all sentient beings. In general terms we recall that each and every one has been our own mother in a previous life. They have fed and protected us and we are in debt to them. In particular, from the very beginning our mind has been unborn and open. It is spacious like the infinite sky. It is where we encounter all beings including ourselves. We are all the radiance of the dharmakaya. As such we are equal however diverse our appearances are. This connectivity is intrinsic and cannot be broken by deluded concepts. Avalokiteshvara manifests the warmth of the Buddha's heart, saying, we are in it together. Even if you want to continue in your delusion that you are not a part of what is going on and you place yourself apart on the outside, you are still on the inside. All sentient beings are already in the mandala of the buddha. Being empty of inherent existence, not one of us is truly apart from everyone else. The fact that we tell lies to ourselves doesn't make the lie true.

The third line says, **"You are the father who gives rise to all the buddhas of the three times."** Generally speaking, in Tibetan Buddhism wisdom is feminine, and compassion or method is the aspect of the masculine, or the father. The mother and the father belong together. If you only have wisdom and no compassion, you can have a very cold clarity, and if you only have a loving kindness, you can stay in a state of agitation because there are so many horrible things happening in the world. It is said that wisdom and compassion are like the two wings of a bird since both need to work in harmony in order for us to fly to enlightenment. However in actual practice we need to open to the understanding of emptiness in order for compassion to be fresh, self-purifying and self-releasing.

As we know, wisdom is invisible, just as women are often invisible. With the rise of feminism we become aware that the feminine principle and the social presence of women are often not privileged and not honoured. Very often in patriarchal society the man comes first. The man sits in the centre of the house, in charge, wearing the clothes washed by the woman, eating the food cooked by the woman. Patriarchy tries to establish a false autonomy; the man standing alone, the father of the people. Where is mum? In the kitchen! Patriarchy, which is to say method expanding to dominate and obscure space, seeks monologue, assertion, control. Whereas, if we start from space, from open availability we realise that we need space to move, that we move in space, facilitated by space – and so we remain respectful of space. We need to awaken to open emptiness if we are to promote the softening of method so that it collaborates rather than dominates. In the images of the deities in sexual union known as yab-yum, father-mother, the male is depicted as much larger than the female. She is hanging on to him – yet her yoni vagina is enveloping his lingam penis. Method moves within the welcoming space of the wisdom of emptiness.

Method is linking and connection; it is the energy of manifestation. With the three aspects or bodies of the buddha, the dharmakaya, the enlightened mind of the buddha is the house of the mother. The two form aspects, the sambhogakaya and the nirmanakaya are activity, the house of the father. If activity is not grounded in emptiness there will be problems. In our practice it is vital to see the infinite emptiness we move within and are never apart from. Our mind itself is not a thing, it is ungraspable like the sky. The energy of the mind manifests as thoughts, feelings, memories, plans, sounds, words, songs, gestures, postures, activities. All these manifestations arise for us as experience: either as direct experience or as experience mediated by concepts. As direct experience they are self-arising and self-liberating. As indirect experience they are understood in terms of self and other, embedded in narratives about what is taken to be occurring.

Samsara is the domain of indirect experience in which appearance is reified and so the agency or method by which these appearances are shaped is privileged. This is the ego as doer and maker, ego as the orphan who has lost his mother and so has to pretend to be big and strong. This sad situation will continue until we once again meet our mother. Then duality and the need to control and dominate will dissolve.

But in order to meet our mother we have to belong to the same family, the family of emptiness. So if we are layered with accretions and burdened with beliefs, we have to shed this load. This can be done quickly or slowly. The quick way is simply to relax free of all that has encumbered you, like easing off a rucksack after a long walk. If you stop carrying it, it is just there and you are free. Now you see that the rucksack was not full of things you needed. It was just a site of experiences – each of which was ungraspable and never 'yours'. Or slowly, we take refuge and develop the bodhisattva intention, then we recognise our tendencies and the harm we have caused, then we purify this by relying on Vajrasattva. Then we pray to our path deity with devotion and receive the white, red and blue lights revealing the empty appearance we are. Then the body of light of the deity dissolves into your body, which is now light, and this unified ball of light gets smaller and smaller until it vanishes into nothing. We rest in that openness. Nothing at all. Not subject, not object. Then from that state experience starts to occur. This is the moment to remember that you love your mama.

What is arising is arising from emptiness. Stay with this clarity otherwise it seems that, "Oh, now I'm back to my familiar world," as you connect with your interpretive concepts and solidify the situation.

So we relax and allow the gradual emergence of patterns inseparable from emptiness. Appearance and emptiness, sound and emptiness, thoughts and feelings inseparable from emptiness. This is the true yab-yum, method within wisdom, the father inside the mother. Emptiness, the womb of the great mother, envelops all forms of manifestation; all movement is moving in the sky-like womb of the mother. If there was no space, there would be no movement. It is the movement of space in space as space. The mother is the infinity within which the various finite moments of method are moving.

If you recall what we looked at earlier, in the first moment of ignoring the openness we have, simultaneously, the imagining of substance. This imagining of substance is the beginning of method operating in duality. There is the subject with agency attempting to get the transient patterning of the potential of the ground to conform to the ego's wishes. It is this alienation of appearance from emptiness, of father from mother, which generates the child of orphaned consciousness. This lonely site of self has to endlessly battle for its own survival only to fail again and again. Like an oedipal triangle, the father sides with the son against the mother so that endless activity in a collapsing world is all that is encountered.

The exit is to release from identification with dualising consciousness and awaken to unborn awareness inseparable from space. The method to achieve this is the minimalist relax and release – a letting go of striving, of agency, of self-creation through activity. There is nothing to do and no one to do it. Deep and open relaxation is free of the dualistic agency of grasping subject and graspable object. Primordial purity is inseparable from effortlessly arising instant presence.

As long as we return to the frame of duality we will be pulled into games of power: winning and losing, fame and notoriety. Then, when we think of another person as someone we can get or use, seeing them as a commodity or as an adorning quality, our relationship with them becomes perverse as does our relationship with ourselves. We become a predator. In the world of politics and in the world of international commerce and finance there are many predators. When hedge funds are gambling on currency rates, they are not concerned with the people whose pay at the end of the week is going to be worth less. To dissolve this kind of cruel and heartless duality we need to develop a sense of inter-subjectivity: you are a subject and I am a subject. You have feelings and I have feelings. Both our feelings, both our thoughts, have validity for us. How can we connect with respect for each other's particularization?

To take the Bodhisattva vow is to say, "*I renounce the objectification of any living creature. I will stay with the bright shining empty vitality of every living creature and encourage them in benign interconnectivity.*" Thus in our verse of homage to Avalokiteshvara, the last line says, we bow in homage to Arya Avalokiteshvara. Instead of Arya we could use the word 'sublime'. The Nazi Party in Germany adopted and perverted some words and symbols (arya, aryan, swastika) so that they are not so easy to use now. Avalokiteshvara is sublime or superior because he doesn't get lost in the world. He sees clearly, quickly, accurately. He sees that all appearance is light. If we can look through his eyes we will see everyone as luminosity, as the light of the ground source. In this way he shows us how to help all sentient beings in the manner of a dream. He does not see real sentient beings who are really suffering and really limited. He sees light shining out of emptiness forming patterns that are blind to their own truth.

The bodhisattva vow in its infinite inclusivity unites insight into emptiness and kindness for all. When this ripens into full enlightenment, the awakening occurs due to merging with mother emptiness, and the subsequent unlimited availability and ceaseless teaching is due to merging with further skilful means.

Generally speaking, we look outside for the light, we look outside for what we need, we look outside at objects. We don't know how to look with ourselves at ourselves so that we see ourselves as we are. We are not looking at thoughts, feelings and all the other experiences we take to be inside our mind. If we do this it is likely to make them seem real and important. Rather by seeing that all these experiences are fleeting and unreliable we can attend to the mind itself. We need to look inward without looking for an object, to look and receive the truth of how it is. When we see that our own mind is not a thing, not an entity, but the open source of all that we experience whether 'outer' or 'inner', then we see that experience is the display or light of this unborn source. Some people can visualise very easily and have a lot of bright dreams. Other people can hardly visualise and have little sense of dreaming.

However we all have experiences both subtle and gross and these are all the light of the mind.

Although our mind is open and empty of defining content it is the site of all our experience. It is luminous, illuminating all that arises in the moment of its occurrence. This luminosity is the basic potential of the mind, the energy of display which manifests as all the appearances we encounter, including ourselves. We are appearances revealed by intrinsic clarity or luminosity flowing from the open empty source. The mother emptiness is inseparable from the father luminosity which is the potential, the kindness of availability, and together they give rise to the unborn appearances which are our own daily experience. All experience is unborn in its inseparability from the ground source. To see this is to be liberated from the delusion of duality and the endless identification of existents. No appearance or experience has inherent existence. All that appears for us, as us, all that is experienced – people, dreams, cars, memories, apples – all are the appearance of light, of the energy of the five senses imagined as entities. We add names, we add concepts. We are storytellers. We invent even when we believe that we are giving an accurate description of material reality. The real, the reality of the material world is just another kind of story. This does not mean that it is nothing at all.

Neither existent nor non-existent, everything that occurs for us is our experience. The 'objective' is imagined for we can only make contact by means of our mind – whatever we touch, taste, smell, hear or see is experience. Appearances are what we experience and these experiences are inseparable for their empty source. They are illusory, not real; appearance and emptiness, father and mother. The true nature of appearances is luminosity. The empty mind effortlessly displays its own light. This inherent light links all sentient beings. When it shines forth, it is the method of kindness that liberates all. Illusory appearances have illusory qualities – hot/cold, hard/soft, loud/quiet, sweet/sour and so on. It is vital to see this directly. The richness of the variety of experience is no proof of existence, or reality or entity. The whole field of occurrence is undivided as luminosity, and if we see that experience is the flavour of that luminosity then all appearances are manifestly empty of self-substance. In this way we open to the experience of the whole, the intrinsic, the complete, the dzogpachenpo, the truth we have been part of from the beginningless beginning. This primordial connectivity is the basis for the liberation of all beings. Although intrinsically free in primordial purity they awaken to their freedom in immediate presence showing the purity free of all stains.

In western cultures we tend to associate love and kindness with the mother, and, perhaps, wisdom with the father. When we use the term wisdom in the west, we mean the accumulation of knowledge and experience. This is very different from the meaning we have been looking at today. The western notion of wisdom is cumulative, compounded, built up step by step, but the wisdom of emptiness is instant, it is the intrinsic clarity of the open ground source. In buddhism compassion is not a compassion for the poor victim. All beings find themselves where they are according to their karma. Where are they? Of course, we think, now I'm a fish, now I'm a bird, I'm a sentient being in samsara. Yet, actually, fish are swimming in the ocean womb of the Great Mother. Birds are flying in the sky womb of the Great Mother.

The Buddha's first teaching is that there is suffering. However suffering itself doesn't make me a victim. Victimhood belongs to the view of duality and reification – as does the role of the rescuer. In order to be a victim we need to interpret what happens to us as having been caused by someone else: they did this to me and that is why I suffer. To be a victim is not only to suffer, but to lose your dignity, to lose your integrity, to lose your sense of personal agency. The teaching on karma calls us back to our responsibility. All that occurs for me is the ripening of my karma, of the results of my previous activity in many former lives. Judging others, blaming others merely hides the cause of my suffering. Similarly judging self, blaming self merely hides the cause of my suffering. I suffer because I am fused with my belief in duality. I am addicted to my belief in my own autonomy and inherent existence. Managing events in an attempt to optimise what I like and minimise what I don't like will not bring freedom – rather it will chain me to the need for endless effort.

However our life is, whether easy or full of functional limitations such as chronic illness, we fortunate ones who have encountered the dharma have the chance to study and practice. We can learn to recognise our own imaginings and gradually release them until we start to see the actual intrinsic truth. The mind, our mind, is always with us and yet how little attention we pay to it! If we see our own mind we see the union of mother Prajnaparamita and father Avalokiteshvara. Their union is our true potential which we can open to directly through relaxing into unborn awareness or indirectly by developing devotion for the forms of these deities as the manifest clarity of the sambhogakaya. Their support and welcome is always available – the question is how available we are to avail ourselves of their availability?

Everything is equal. Everything is the breath of emptiness. Paths or methods or ways of proceeding are useful, if they are actually used. In principle everything is useful. However, if a method is not useful for you, and yet everybody says, 'Oh, but it is the best, it is the best!', then you should not disparage a method because it does not work for you. The best dharma is always the dharma you actually do. Dharma as theory is not worth an ice cream.

བཀྲ་ཤིས་པའི་དཔལ་རིག་པའི་ཁུ་བྱུག།

THE CUCKOO'S CRY HERALDING THE GOOD FORTUNE OF GLORIOUS PRESENCE

by Vairocana

སྣ་ཚོགས་རང་བཞིན་མི་གཉིས་ཀྱང་།

ཆ་ཤས་ཉིད་དུ་སྤྲོས་དང་བྲལ།

ཇི་བཞིན་བ་ཞེས་མི་རྟོག་ཀྱང་།

རྣམ་པར་སྣང་མཛད་ཀུན་ཏུ་བཟང་།

ཟིན་པས་རྩོལ་བའི་ནད་སྤངས་ཏེ།

ལྷུན་གྱིས་གནས་པས་བཞག་པ་ཡིན།

The infinite diversity of experiences and their actual nature are non-dual.
Yet the actuality of each particular occurrence is beyond judgement.
What is known as 'as it is' is untouched by thought
Yet the forms of appearance are unobstructed, being complete as they are.
Being intact we are free of the sickness of effort,
Spontaneously abiding and so everything is settled.

Diversity and nature non-dual:
Specific apparitions, each beyond judgement.
'As it is', neither concept nor conceptualisable:
All manifesting is perfect, complete in itself.
Intrinsically complete, untouched by the disease of effort:
Spontaneous presence, unchanging.

Diversity essence, non-dual:
Apparitions specific, beyond judgement.
'As it is', not concept, not caught by concept:
Manifest, perfect; the common good.
Complete in itself, the disease of effort discarded:
Spontaneous presence, settled.

This text expresses the view of dzogchen. Written by the Indian scholar yogi, Vairocana, it invites us to the ever-present springtime of fresh awareness. I offer three translations of its six lines in order to give a sense of its density and compactness. The commentary follows the first translation. It is very short yet succinctly outlines the three-fold aspects of the ground/base/source, the path and the result.

THE GROUND

The ground or the base is our actual state. We have never strayed from our basis yet this truth is hidden from us by the hazy delusions which envelop us. However, we are here. How we are here either does or does not reveal our intrinsic clarity. Therefore we have to start with ourselves as we are at this moment. We don't start with analysis or theory, but by opening to how we are. This teaching is like a visit to the optician. The text is going to help our tired eyes to see. Instead of straining we can employ the lens of these few lines to let us see more clearly. We're not going to the clothes shop; we're not getting more garments which we can wrap around ourselves. The immediate direct clarity of awareness is very different from knowing about something. When you know about something your knowledge is based on a pattern of concepts, concepts which are themselves impermanent in their presence in your mind. Due to this impermanence, concept patterns are inherently unreliable. At various stages in our life we have studied in school, college and so on, yet the knowledge that we acquired at that time has become unavailable to us. It was ours, maybe it helped us to pass some exams, but then it dissolved leaving mere traces.

It is for this reason that with dzogchen we are not concerned to build up castles of contingent information. We want to open ourselves to the intrinsic, to our direct presence in the here and now. Thoughts are not the enemy; they are the radiance of the mind. But when we don't see the source of our thoughts they operate together in a constructive fashion fabricating the deceptive imaginary. Believing in the imaginary we find ourselves in a fragmented world composed of many different things.

The text is composed of six lines arranged in three groups of two lines. The first two lines are concerned with the base or ground, followed by two on the path and then two on the result. I have made three different translations of the text to try to bring out some of its flavour.

The title indicates the good fortune of awareness announcing itself like a cuckoo welcoming the spring. The cuckoo announces that winter is truly over, summer is coming, we can relax. This is the central point of our dzogchen practice: to relax into the intrinsic, into how it already is by itself. In the winter of ignorance we tighten up inside and want to protect ourselves against the challenging environment. It is me against the world. But when we feel that spring is here we see that the sun of awareness is brightening the sky. Now it is more pleasant to walk outside, there are wild flowers, and we feel relaxed as part of the world. This is the flavour of the title: to trust that it is okay to open to the openness that is everywhere.

The first line, **'The infinite diversity of experiences and their actual nature are non-dual'**, reminds us that we and our life and our world are in fact composed of many, many kinds of experiences. When we look around we see such variety: our own possessions and the trees and the cars and people, dogs and so on. They look like different things. They seem to have different qualities and different functions. Through our education we've learned how to name these things in various ways. We have the sense that the name is applied to something, that the something-ness of the world was there before the name, so that even if we didn't know the name, the thing itself would still be there existing in itself. Due to experiencing the world in this way we encounter a whole lot of stuff. Yet when we pay attention we will see that the diversity of phenomena or objects or commodities or entities is actually a diversity of experience. There are no different things and commodities, what we actually encounter is the diversity of our experience. Experience is the mind's self-revelation. It can be dulled by reification or we can awaken to this ceaseless display which sometimes seems subject and sometimes seems object. Awareness reveals the ever-open space within which 'self' and 'world' are co-emergent. The term 'world' points to an untotalisable potential, a potential which is revealed in co-emergence with the potential of self. Both, world or environment, are beyond conceptual grasp. They are the immediacy of this specific patterning only available in this moment of the here and now. The same applies to 'self'. Self is not something I have or am; 'self' points to the site of my experience of this moment of the here and now.

Both are infinite and ungraspable and so whatever is said about them is mere fallen leaves from the evergreen tree of life.

The actual nature or how-it-is-ness of whatever is occurring is not different from how it shows. There are no specific essences or existents behind the showing. All that is seen, heard and so on is the showing of the potential of empty awareness. Every appearance is not some-thing which we experience – experience is the union of subject and object or experiencer and experienced. Moreover experience occurs here and now, not in the past, not in the future … but just this … direct and immediate. When you think about 'the experience', when you apply a conceptual elaboration, it is as if the past and the future can exist as two structures which you can visit. You can think about the past, you can think about the future, as if they were available somewhere. The past, present, and future do not exist. They are concepts which refract the instant moment and seem to fracture time into these three fragments. The actual present moment is not to be found within these three – although paradoxically these three are actually only within the present moment. Time in its actuality cannot be comprehended in any way. The concepts we use to comprehend it are an aspect of delusion. Time is presence, the moment that is actually occurring is always now. Thus it is not that you can go to the past, or go to the future; the past and the future and the conceptual present are moods or flavours of now.

The openness of the ground source, the emptiness of the ground source, and what is occurring are not dual, they are not two different things. Non-duality doesn't mean that different things have been brought together. From the very beginning the ground source, the inconceivable infinity of the mind, is not other than all that appears. The unborn ungraspable mind is the source of everything because every 'thing' is in fact ungraspable experience, self-arising and self-vanishing in the manner of a dream. In this way, the diversity of all that can occur, all that is experienced, is not other than its own nature of emptiness. Everything that appears is the appearance of no-thing. There is nothing to get, nothing to reject. There is neither lack nor excess. Our mind is not improved by 'good' thoughts and feelings, and it is not defiled by 'bad' thoughts and feelings. How it is, is how it is. How it is, is not 'something' to be discovered by analysis. It is as it is, just this. Fully here and fully gone. This is not a problem to be solved nor is it a mystery to be lived. By releasing our dualising consciousness from the task of 'sorting things out', consciousness has no object and thins to a fine summer cloud into the clear open sky of awareness.

This is the great completion, the intrinsic primordial completion. There has never been any separation or fragmentation or creation. Whatever occurs is inseparable from the unborn mind. Whose mind? Our mind. Why do we not see this? Because we think we know what our mind is. Some people think that their mind is their brain and become very excited by neuroscience. Some people think that their mind is very bright or very dull, for they see it in terms of its cognitive capacity. Some people think of their mind in terms of their feelings, and so they become suffused with sadness or happiness. But if we stay with this word 'experience', it points to occurrence or happening. Appearing is a verb, showing is a verb. These are dynamic; the self-arising and self-vanishing is almost simultaneous and not one single entity is ever established. The appearance has no self-substance and it is not other than the luminous space of appearance.

However if experience is reified then our experience is thickened by the thought that something is happening, something is occurring. And then, from that a further thought establishes that 'something is happening to me, or for me'. This is an artificial elaboration, you are making sense of what is going on by interpreting it in terms of your individual ego-self. This is the false base or the false ground: I am me, I have always been me, I am like an irreducible substance; and what I want from the world, what I want to do and where I want to go depends on this sense of I, me, myself.

Since my way of appearing is co-emergent with the circumstances I am participating with what actually occurs since what I take to be 'I, me, myself', is always changing. This self is an idea, it is a concept. Concepts are sticky. They adhere to each other. We know this through language and its flow as narrative sequence. We tell stories about what is going on, we talk about something. In fact we talk 'some-things' into existence. They seem to exist for us because we believe in them. If there are no some-things, language loses its employment. The task of language is to mediate the world of things. Yet transcendent discernment, the wisdom of emptiness, is inexpressible. We need to speak and to hear in order to develop some understanding, but this conceptual understanding is like scaffolding. You can use scaffolding to create a building, but you can also use it to take down the building.

In our daily life we are busy with the task of construction. We make stories to live in, stories of our identity. We make stories to allocate value to the entities we believe that we encounter. Moreover we incorporate aspects of other people's stories into our own stories and in this way our stories become more comprehensible to others.

But when we start to apply the view of dzogchen to our experience we see that all our constructs, all the products of our effort that we rely on, are in fact unborn illusions. Now we can start to release ourselves from our habitual tendency to concretize the illusory. We can use the scaffolding of dharma as a temporary site from which to observe how the walls we have constructed, the walls of separation and evaluation, will start to come down by themselves. As the first line indicates, the true actuality of everything is open and empty and ungraspable.

When we simply relax and release ourselves from our habitual beliefs, we see that all appearance is and remains unconstructed and so it self-vanishes. We don't need to purify the world. There are no real existent things to obscure or obstruct the free flow of illusory appearance. When we see that what we take to be 'the world out there' is in fact the play of the mind, a theatre of illusion, a magician's construct, we can truly let go. The magician has not constructed anything, but their skill in deception brings us into believing that they have made something. Oh, now I get it!

The second line states, **"Yet the actuality of each particular occurrence is beyond judgement."** Look around your room and randomly choose any item – shoes, cup of coffee, whatever it is. "This is a cup of coffee"– this is an interpretation, this is how you relate to what is in front of you. Your experience is being mediated through your conceptual capacity. You believe the concepts. 'Cup of coffee' is a concept. It is a way of naming something. As soon as the naming fixes the object our judgements start to arise: it is delicious, it is terrible. These judgements become our focus of attention and mediate our experience—thus further veiling the bright actuality. This process starts from the assumption that there is something there, an object that can be seen and known. Actually light is appearing - what you see is a pattern of light. Maybe the cup is white and the coffee inside is black. White and black are words. Different languages express the perceived difference in different ways. The actual, the revelation, is beyond concepts in its immediacy. It is beyond comparing and contrasting. Yet the ego-self feels a necessity, an urge to name and define – just as the ego itself is nothing other than the naming and defining of transient patterning, shape and colour are identified as features of the flow when in fact they are concepts imposed on the flow. Light is flow, yet 'cup of coffee' seems to freeze the flow of light and substantialize it as a true entity. If you see this, then you see that, then you see that the actuality is unspeakable, inexpressible. There is not something there to get hold of, it is revelation beyond judgement.

Beyond judgement indicates that the attribution of qualities to this seeming object is a movement of the energy of the mind. Moreover the prior judgement that there is some existent there, is a parallel movement of the energy of the mind. Both the seeming existence of the cup and the attributions we place on it are merely the movements of our mind and do not reveal the actuality of empty appearance. When I say that I know it is a cup of coffee, what I am claiming is that I exist as an observer, as an experiencer, as a knower, separate from what is observed, experienced and known. The identification of the object is based on it being other than the subject. I know myself and I stand in my opinion. I don't care what you think or what you say. For me it is a cup of coffee.

Here we can see that the open actual ungraspable ground is hidden by our addiction to the formulation of a false ground, a ground of imagined real existents. I think I am in touch with the actual but in fact I'm in touch with a fabrication, something artificial, and I am taking this construct to be a self-existing existent. This is a false, deceptive, mutant intrinsicality. The true intrinsic is always effortlessly here and now, it just is. But when we elaborate our judgements, it is like a game of tennis: you move energy towards the object and the object seems to move energy back towards you. I know it is a cup of coffee, and the coffee confirms to me in its truth that I am someone who knows something. This is a game of mental dullness. It looks like light, it looks like my intelligence lets me know what this is, but the solidification hides the actuality that what is appearing is light.

Thus the latter part of the second line points to how our ordinary sense of the world is interpretation structured through polarities established by mutual exclusion. Implicit in the assertion that this is a cup of coffee is the certainty that it is not a cup of tea. The non-tea-ness of this cup is its coffee-ness. When something is asserted, simultaneously something else is being non-asserted or dispensed with. If it is high, it is not low, if it is male, it is not female. The polarities establish the isolation of the item referred to by the exclusion of all that is not it. However this line is pointing out that this way of formulating, of understanding, is an artificial construct which is not to be found in the actuality of how things are. When we look at the cup of coffee, if we don't say 'cup of coffee', we still think, well there's something there. What is that something? It is a porcelain cup or a cheap cup. Oh, I am saying this, I am adding this. What is this cup in itself? Well, it is white in colour, I say. Is it white in colour for a pig or a fish? The whiteness of the white exists as our interpretation. It is a mental activity projected into the object, and then reflected back to the subject as if it were inherent.

When you stop projecting meaning into the object and leave it as it is, it has no hooks for concepts. It is smooth like a billiard ball. There are no corners. You turn it and you can't find top or bottom, inside or outside. In itself, intrinsically, it is free from any concept which can be applied to it. When you apply the concept, you blind yourself to how it is in itself and give birth to how it is for you. Then, it is as if it is the way I think it is. It is not actually this, but this is how I believe it to be. And because we are social creatures and use language, we learn what is the socially acceptable way of interpreting this seeming thing. I'm not setting this out as some kind of analysis you have to repeatedly do, but simply to point out that we arrive at the conclusion that 'this is a cup of coffee' on the basis of a lot of mental activity. So, now perhaps we can see why the instruction in dzogchen is always to relax. Do less!

This doesn't mean sitting on the sofa and daydreaming. It means staying relaxed in the unborn openness of your mind as various thoughts, feelings, sensations and so on arise. The clarity of simple openness to what is being revealed has no need of involvement. It abides in evenness, satisfied with neither lack nor excess. With this state of awareness each thought that arises is like a window cleaner, removing the adventitious accumulation which has never penetrated or sullied the window itself. As the thoughts, feelings and so on arise and pass, the non-involved mind becomes brighter. However, if one falls into involvement with the thought, and takes this thought to be a messenger of truth, then we are likely to be drawn towards a solidifying conclusion, "Oh, this coffee smells very good, it must be the Arabica bean." Now you can add more of your knowledge about the history and geography of coffee production into this poor little cup.

In meditation this occurs when we get distracted by following the thought and imagine that it can add value to our life. If you then notice that you got distracted and judge that you shouldn't fall into the thought, you will struggle to stay clear! Unfortunately the clarity established by this dualistic analysis and effort is transient. So rather than judging whether one is distracted or not, stay open and present with the mind however it is arising. The movement of the mind and the stillness of the mind are not two things which can be pulled apart. The stillness of the mind, its simple awareness, is present even in distraction. It is the ego's willingness to be distracted that brings the intensity of the fusion of subject and object, from which arises mental dullness. This intoxication makes openness to awareness hard to open to although it is always available right now.

The term non-duality indicates that how you actually are and how you appear are not two separate domains. All of samsara, all entities, things, people, mountains, computers are simply experiences reified into the delusion of items having inherent existence. Not one atom of an entity has ever actually occurred. They are modes of emptiness and as such have no self-substance. Thus all our imaginings, how we take empty appearances to be things, can create no actual things. The actual and the imagined are equal in their unborn emptiness. However arisings occur, in whatever form or intensity, they are non-dual with their own actuality. This actuality is their ungraspability, their unborn insubstantiality.

When we talk of the ground you might think of the earth outside. If you want to build a house you make foundations and then you build something up stage by stage. The house is other than the earth, it stands in relation to the earth. There are two things: the earth and the house. But in dzogchen the terms 'base' or 'ground' or 'source' are concerned with the actual, the immediate, not the constructed, the imagined, the conceptual. In this first line Vairocana is pointing out that the diversity of experience, all possible occurrences, from the highest to the lowest, in any country, in any language, for fish, for ducks, for any sentient being, have never been created, have never been born. They are not things, they are not entities. As an example, consider a rainbow. We see the rainbow, the rainbow is there. Yet the rainbow is not a thing. It is an illusion; the illusion is something ungraspable. It is in the sky, it is not separated from the sky. You can't take the rainbow out of the sky. It is not in opposition to the sky nor is it other than the sky.

Non-duality collapses the substantial basis of all polarities and binaries. The words and concepts are still usable but now we see that they are a rainbow-like formation within the infinity of the sky-like mind. Moreover, there is not just one thing, nor are there many different things. All possible appearances are fundamentally, intrinsically, free of the least existence or relativity. Whether smell or taste or sound or touch, all such phenomena are inseparable from this open ground. They are not born, yet they can appear to be born when we engage in conceptual identification. The use of concepts gives us the sense that I can catch or take hold of whatever is arising, although in itself it is ungraspable.

It is vital to see that our ego-self is a concept and that its power derives from its impacting and influencing other concepts. By adopting and rejecting conceptual interpretations of what is occurring the ego attempts to control the patterning of its experience. This delusion of autonomy and personal power is an intoxicating deception that keeps us powerfully impotent: powerful within duality yet impotent to escape duality.

For example, if I look out my window, I can say, "That car is blue." Blue takes two seconds to say. The word arises and vanishes. This is how it manifests. Yet the word blue seems to plug into an eternal blue-ness, so that it seems that I am saying something definite about the enduring colour of the car. Because it has been raining a lot in London, the car I am looking at is covered in drops of water. What I see is some shining moments, shining drops of the water on a glistening surface. That is how it is. So, when I say 'blue', I claim the existence of a permanent quality irrespective of the rain. Similarly, I can ignore how the car is partly in the shadow of a tree, so that some part is bright and some part is not. If I ignore the rain and the shadow and simply state, "it is blue, it is always blue", then I privilege the conceptual, the mediated, over the immediate. Concepts are the food of the ego. The ego is itself a concept, and the more I use concepts the more 'I' as a concept am strengthened. However, the diversity of appearance is inseparable from its own ungraspability, and so there is no actual basis for judgement. Clarity is this showing, just as it is. Clarity is present before, during and after conceptual interpretation. Conceptual interpretation moves through clarity without disturbing it, in the way clouds move through the sky. But we can only see the true nature of clouds when we see how the sky is – and likewise we only see the true nature of arisings when we see how clarity, our mind is.

With the Dzogchen view we integrate sitting practice and being in the world. Resting in the bright receptivity of open awareness we are available as instant presence all the time. Whether we are walking or talking or eating or sleeping, we do not stray from the infinite openness of the mind itself. We do not block the movement of the mind, and nor do we settle on the movement of the mind. We practise in order to dissolve the boundary between sitting and moving. We sit in open clarity and we move in the field of clarity. As I get up from where I am sitting, I become aware of the muscles tensing and releasing. I move according to the placement of furniture in the room. My body is revelation within the field of revelation, as are the floor, the walls, the books and the door. The body is revealed as movement; it is turning as it negotiates its way out of the room, and the room is revealing itself, moment-by-moment, as my head turns, as I turn in order to go out. If we abide in the presence of open awareness there is the undivided clarity of illusory forms beyond conceptualisation.

I am part of the integrity of the display of the field of experience. I am only made to seem apart from it through reliance on concepts. Here there is a great paradox: my sense of myself as an isolated creature is a mental construction, an interpretation, and yet these concepts have no other source than the open empty radiance of the mind. So, the imagining which brings me to the sense of 'I am just me' is the same imagining that says, 'this is a cup of coffee.' These are ideas moving in the space of the mind. When these ideas move together, they generate pattern after pattern after pattern. If viewed from the standpoint of the ego-self what we encounter is seen in terms of identification, judgement, polarities and all the conceptual tools with which we try to sort it all out. Once you think that this world is 'stuff', then you have to work out what kind of stuff is here. To do so, we rely on polarities. Thus, outside the window I can see an expensive big new car and an old, probably second-hand car, which leads me to think, some people in the street have more money than others ... and more thoughts and more thoughts can be brought in to elaborate the picture that confirms that I know what is going on.

All compositional factors are themselves non-dual with and unseparated from the actuality of the diversity of appearance. When this is not clear for me I make trouble for myself. The base, unchanging openness, is the source of both samsara and nirvana. From the base, the ground of our actuality, uncreated, ungraspable, uncompounded presence arises in the manner of a dream. Like magical creations, both awareness and non-awareness arise while remaining unarisen. The openness of the mind itself has no bias. The mind itself is open to whatever comes – it does not judge or select. For openness, clarity is not 'better' than delusion. The open mind is free of reliance on hierarchy, polarity and judgement. Whatever comes, comes. Whatever goes, goes. Only awareness is open to this. The ego-self cannot access its own ground since its false ground, its belief in its real existence, is the rejection of its true actual ground. We often find ourselves on the path of unawareness; we are busy in our constructive activity. From the dualistic point of view this is an error and we need to make effort to change. With the non-dual view of dzogchen we see that busyness and self-absorption are inseparable from the relaxed open ground. We haven't strayed, we haven't gone anywhere else, we haven't fallen out of heaven into hell.

Let's just sit for a little bit. Sit with your skeleton carrying your weight. Our gaze is open. We're not staring at anything, simply resting our gaze in space. Gaze open, senses open, mind open: movement is unobstructed. Sensations arise and pass, reifying convictions such as 'I am here as an enduring self' arise and pass. Whenever there is a sensation or a thought that seems to confirm, 'I'm here, always just me', don't merge into it as if it is true and don't stand apart from it as if it is something toxic. Simply stay relaxed and open, whatever arises.

The awareness present in sitting and the awareness present in moving are not different. Whether making a cup of tea or simply sitting, thoughts, feelings, and sensations come and go; experience is occurring in the space of the mind. When you stand up and do different activities, this is all just experience moving in the space of awareness. The infinite diversity of these experiences is inseparable from the open ground. Given that we live as this body, hot and cold are different experiences which make a difference to us. If you make a coffee and it is very hot, you have to drink it carefully, otherwise your mouth will be burned. However, this is not because the coffee is real, your mouth is real and the burning sensation is real. The intensity of an experience is not an indicator as to whether it is 'real' or not. Pain and pleasure are both experiences and one is not more real than the other. Our body is not a thing – it is an interactive patterning. Its integrity is relational; it is not guaranteed by an internal essence. For example, if you drink the coffee quickly and you burn your lip, then for the next hour or so your lip is going to be sensitive and then the heightened sensation starts to fade. Thus experience leads to experience, leads to experience. There are no fixed entities. So, rest in the unchanging while experience ceaselessly changes.

THE PATH

The next two lines of this short text are concerned with the path. In dzogchen the path is simply not to stray from the view. We are familiar with our karmic paths which are how we come to be here in this place together. Although we are always already in the here and now, due to our impulses and obscurations we travel off in our thoughts and memories and plans, so that even when we are here, we believe we're not here. This is our lostness.

To awaken us from this, Vairocana reminds us that what is known as 'as it is', is untouched by thought. 'As it is' indicates unchanging open awareness. This is not some kind of a pure domain which is going to be spoiled by the arising of thought and experience. For example, the mirror is filled with reflections yet the reflection doesn't spoil the mirror, doesn't touch the mirror. When we turn the mirror, new reflections arise. There is no trace of the previous reflection. Similarly, although experience is ceaseless, it is self-arising and self-liberating and leaves no trace. If it is grasped at, it cannot be caught. However as with some lizards – if you catch their tail they release and run away leaving you with the tail – when an emergent thought is grasped at, it self-liberates leaving you with the concept of it – which is not the actual thought.

The third line, **"What is known as 'as it is' is untouched by thought"** indicates that our open awareness will not be damaged by any kind of experience. Awareness is often referred to as vajra, indestructible. It has no substance at all and does not stand in relation to any occurrence. If you have an accident and break your leg you have some pain. You can't walk very well, you feel different, you don't feel happy. You might have thoughts such as, 'Why did this happen to me, how could I be so stupid, why, why did they behave like that and cause me to fall over?" This is thoughts chasing thoughts. In this text the word 'thought' also indicates sensations, emotions, memories. It means all kinds of experiences. I, the ego-self, am upset that my leg is broken. I am experiencing difficulties. However, my unborn awareness is not. It is not self-referential. Awareness is simply aware – neither involved in nor reactive towards diverse experiences. On the basis of the pain, I think "Poor me, how I suffer!" My experience of events and my experience of me are mutually influencing, yet the clarity of the mind revealing what is occurring is not touched by any of this. "Should I be brave with my broken leg or should I cry a lot and ask people to look after me?" That will depend on how much of me the people around me can bear to experience. They will have a limited capacity to experience poor little Jimmy. At a certain point they say, "Hey, get over it!" Our ego-self is limited and it imposes limitations on both self and others. This is the patterning of how our energy manifests. It is vital not to identify with the patterning of our habitual self.

The self is a transient site of experiencing, arising and passing in the field of awareness. It has no fixed content and its seeming continuity is merely the application of the concepts, 'I, me, myself' to diverse moments of experience. So as beginners we have to release and relax again and again. Release from identification with the concept of self and relax into the open welcome of ever-present awareness. The mirror shows beautiful images, ugly images, horrifying images. The mirror itself does not become horrifying by being placed in front of some horrifying image. It merely shows the horrifying reflection without itself being horrified. Similarly our indestructible base, the non-duality of awareness and open emptiness, shows everything without being touched. It is not defensively standing apart. It does not stand anywhere. It is always simply here and now and every possible experience is non-dual with it. Whatever occurs awareness remains open and unaffected. So whenever you find yourself caught up in identification with thoughts, feelings and memories, don't take this as something bad. Don't enter into judgement. Don't take the event as an object and your consciousness of it as the subject. If you relax free of your dualistic fixation, your dualising consciousness will be thinned of defining content and 'knowing something' will be revealed as transient experience by 'simply knowing' which now shines forth. Simply stay present with what is occurring, neither merging nor avoiding.

When you look in the mirror you see your reflection. If you are very involved then the reflection will seem to be you – you are looking at yourself. Now, just relax back a little and see, 'Oh, this is an image in the mirror, and, oh, the mirror is on the wall.' What I was sure was 'me' is now clearly just a transient reflection. It was not a real entity. It doesn't have to be taken out of the mirror. It doesn't damage the mirror. The mirror can remain open and relaxed throughout the intimate presence of the reflection. This clarity is precisely what we are opening to in our practice. Thoughts arise in the mind the way reflections arise in the mirror. Neither mind nor mirror is affected. But reflections impact other reflections, and my experience of others impacts my experience of myself. I am an experience appearing amidst all the other experiences that are revealed by clarity. The ego-self does not have to be altered, removed or destroyed. It does not exist. The error lies in believing in it as an existent, a special existent, the existent of I, me, myself.

When it is clear that I am not a separate self then self is seen to be apparitional patterning within the field of clarity: I am open and empty; I am clear and luminous; I am apparitional patterning. This presence is without bias or prejudice. Free of lack and excess it is even in all circumstances. It abides in non-dual equanimity towards all the dreamlike experiences that effortlessly come and go. The 'how it is' of each occurrence is inseparable from the 'as it is' truth or actuality of its base, our ever-open awareness.

There is no need to do anything special or go anywhere else. Each messy thought and the melange of feelings and sensations is always inseparable from awareness. Open to it, relax with it. Samsara is unborn. It is an illusion. It abides with it in the infinite hospitality of the dharmadhatu, the space of occurrence. All entities are imagined. They are delusions which have no inherent existence and so there are no negative occurrences to be blocked and no positive occurrences to be encouraged. The unborn is untouched by gain or loss. The eight worldly concerns have no impact on it. It is the actually-unborn-yet-imagined-born-and-existent-ego that is buffeted by gain and loss, success and failure, fame and notoriety, praise and blame. Relax and open and you will find yourself to be not other than the intrinsic completion of Samantabhadra. All experience is in itself momentary and complete.

The fourth line of our text, **"Yet the forms of appearance are unobstructed, being complete as they are."** indicates that everything is radiance and everything is good. We have no access to anything without our mind. Our world is what arises for us. Even if you think of another planet and you imagine alien creatures living on that planet, you haven't left your own mind. We can imagine the centre of the earth, we can imagine the distant limits of the universe. What we imagine is our experience. We can experience through the senses. We also experience ideas. As we have already discussed, all experience can be direct immediacy or indirect conceptualisation, the Tibetan words in this line indicate illumination and perfection. If you enter into a cognitive interpretation of an experience, then you string together many different ideas and make a story. And if you believe in this story it will wrap you in it and hide the simple actuality. Stay with the freshness of the immediate!

In our experience of being sentient beings wandering in samsara, identifying with dualised self and other, we seek connectivity in order to survive and, if possible, to thrive. We seek contact with others as their 'existence' seems to confirm our 'existence'. All of the experiences which arise in this way are not, in their truth and immediacy, what we take them to be. The ungraspable immediate is of no use to the ego-self. The ego-self seeks the graspable. It therefore grasps ideas, concepts, the residue of the immediate – the mere naming of the ghosts and echoes of the already vanished. Thinking about what you think about what the other person meant when they said something to you is like wandering in a maze. Yet if you simply stay present with the arising and vanishing of a thought you are being offered a moment of clarity.

Each moment is complete as it is. This is the primordial Buddha, Samantabhadra, the 'all-good'. As it is, everything is good; everything is perfectly just what it is. If you have a broken leg, you have a broken leg. It is what it is. This is the dzogchen path, to be with how it is as it is. If no arousal occurs, if there is no dualistic judgement and reaction – 'this is terrible!' – then this is simply this pattern of experience. It is an unexpected set of circumstances so the task is not to generate opinions about it but to see how it is and to work with these circumstances. If you have a love story with someone and it goes bad, you have a broken heart. This broken heart is a perfect broken heart. It is simply broken, that's all. You cry. Why would you not cry! It is what it is. If you stay present with it as it is, there is the immediate vitality of the situation. This is fresh. It is not a story. If you develop a story about it and tell your friends the story it takes on a life of its own and working with the actual circumstances becomes more difficult. Stay with the immediacy and when it vanishes there is no trace. It is the story that leaves traces. So, stay present in the moment, it is how it is. Just this! Not going after the past, not waiting expectantly for the future. This is the great simplicity, the great completion, the great perfection. The actual is not complicated. Complication arises from our own thought process. The ego is hungry for importance, and it finds this by inserting doubts and hesitancy and worry and anxiety. In this way the simplicity of immediacy is not attended to.

If we remember Garab Dorje's three key instructions: the first is to open to the open; the second is to not remain in doubt (don't take up a position, is it right, is it wrong, don't think about it); and the third is to continue in this way. All three are saying: keep it simple. Stay with the 'as is' and maintain the 'as if' within the 'as is'.

Our texts often point out that if you go to a land of gold, all you will find is gold. So here you are in the land of great perfection, the land of gold, and yet the thought arises, is there any silver here? You are disturbing yourself with thoughts about how it could be rather than how it actually is. Gold is gold. We are gold in the land of gold. We are the radiance of the pure ground, the infinite source. We are the presence of the clarity of awareness inseparable from emptiness which manifests these fields of illusory appearance. Do not doubt that gold is gold. Do not imagine that there is something better than this. This is the truth of all appearance so do not be misled by your own erroneous imaginings. All of samsara is imagined so do not follow the elaboration of imaginings but rather see the ground of all these imaginings for that ground is the pure gold source of the gold that is everywhere. Gold is greatly appreciated because of its value and for the way it can be shaped and moulded into infinite designs. The diversity of appearances is the rich potential of this golden source.

Light is shining everywhere yet we don't see the light as light, we see the light when it illuminates an appearance. Luminosity or clear light is the invisible light whose potential is released as the five colours (white, yellow, red, green and blue) which manifest the five elements, the five poisons, and the five wisdoms. The ungraspable ground potential manifests all the rich variety of appearance. If we see this then the true nature of all appearance is obvious. This is how it is, no matter how it looks. But if we do not see this then we want to know what it is. We apply names and interpretations in our effort to gain clarity but all we are doing is increasing the opacity of what we encounter. Without recognising it we are on the road to darkness, to obscuration, to consolidation.

Therefore it is vital to follow Garab Dorje's teaching and see one's own face, the primordial ground from which and as which every appearance arises. Then our life can be quite light and free. Even when we are sad, our practice is to see the sadness as arising in the open sky of awareness. Then, without altering or antidoting the sadness we remain relaxed and open. Sadness comes, loneliness comes, jealousy comes – so many different moods. When we see that they go then when they come we don't feel trapped or conditioned by this transient event. Problems arise when we try to resist what is occurring, "I don't want it! I want my life to be different, this shouldn't be happening to me!" By setting ourselves against what is occurring we adopt an ego-identification and the actions we take to manage the situation alienates us from our own ground. The ego-self construct is fragile and often feels, "I am not able to be present with life as it is because my image of myself feels insulted or defiled by this emergent experience." However, my image of myself, my shape of myself, is also an emergent moment. There is no fixed self. Each form we call 'I, me, myself' is also already vanishing. It arises, shows, and vanishes within the expanse of inexpressible open awareness.

The whole which is the great completion is never divided. It doesn't split into polarities or parts, and yet within this infinite whole there is infinite diversity. The diversity doesn't mean separation from the whole, it is the inclusive richness of the whole. The path is this: whatever is arising in your life, however it is, stay relaxed and open, and it will pass. However if the congealing and thickening ego-self puts itself forward as the owner of the experience, then you have problems. You have lost your own ground, you have substituted it with the pseudo ground of the enduring self-entity. Everything has the same source. There is no other factory creating ego-entities. The sense of self-existing entities is delusion. Illusion arises from the ground. Why does it do this? It has no reason to do it. There is no doer, there is no god, no big papa, no creator with a divine plan. It arises as a happenstance which, if you stay present, is the bright clarity of the ground. But if you retreat into your small imitation of god, "I am the maker, I am the owner", this is the delusional ego. "It is my life, I'll lead it the way I want to!" This mad assertion is the path to suffering.

After birth we find ourselves in this life. As a small child, you gradually become conscious of your body. If you bang your head it hurts. You find yourself within a world that was there before you were born. It is true, you came out of your mother's body, but your mother's body was already in the world, as part of the world. You are part of the world, this world which actually is the radiance of ungraspable awareness.

The Result

The final two lines of our short text are concerned with the result. **"Being intact we are free of the sickness of effort,"** Intact, undamaged, unharmed, indicates that we are part of the whole; we are a flavour or pattern of the emergence of the potential of the ground. Our ground is our empty awareness. We rest in this ground as simultaneously its potential emerges as our own interactive patterning. We follow the middle way: we are not the master of the situation, and we are not the victim of the situation. We are working with circumstances while manifesting in the field of connectivity. The connectivity is intrinsic. When you are present in and as awareness of the ground, you do not have to make effort to integrate. Everything is already integrated. What we have to do is to avoid slipping into the delusion of disintegration.

The result is that we abide in unborn awareness in all circumstances. Awareness is like the mirror; appearance is like the reflection in the mirror. The mirror doesn't move. We sit in the practice, open and relaxed – and suddenly we are merged in movement. It is as if we have fallen out of the state of the mirror into the reflection. It is as if we have fallen out of the state of the sky into a cloud. It is as if we have fallen out of the state of awareness into a thought. No one has fallen. It is a momentary distraction, a slippage which has not taken us anywhere else – for there is nowhere other than the integrity of here and now. Relax. Relax. Relax. Arousal and involvement will transform a blip into a problem and this will evoke ego-centric thoughts and feelings – and in this blizzard of arisings you will be pushed and pulled and lose your openness to the ever-open.

Something arises and is taken as the object. It has an impact, pleasurable or unpleasurable, and so there is a reaction. I push it away or I pull it towards me. Who is the doer of this movement? This is a swirl of energy for there are no self-existing entities. There is always and forever an absence of inherent existence in whatever occurs. So, it is not that I become distracted and I go after a thought. That is a dualistic interpretation. Of course, it makes sense to us because we live most of the time in duality, unfortunately. But if you imagine your mind to be like the open ocean, a wave arises, followed by another wave, and more waves going up and down rolling along. The first wave is an object-side wave, the second is a subject-side wave. These are waves of energy or manifestation of the open ground. The wave is not separate from the ocean. It is always part of the ocean. Even if you're out amongst the waves, you are a wave; you are a wave, and each wave of 'you' is already vanishing as the ocean. Because even as the wave arises it is the ocean arising. The wave is how the ocean shows itself. Each thought is like a wave of the infinite ocean mind. The thought is not other than the mind yet not identical with it since it has its momentary specific form. This is how we are: awareness and emptiness, clarity and emptiness, appearance and emptiness.

So, when we sit in relaxed openness without any agenda or aim, whatever occurs, however it occurs, is just the non-dual movement of the mind. There is nothing to judge, nothing to change, nothing to adopt or reject. In this openness free of fixation, distraction is impossible; just arising and passing of illusory patterns inseparable from the unborn ground – that is all! Awareness doesn't move, it reveals movement. The ego-self is an ever-changing patterning of the movement of illusion; these movements are always dissolving. Already today each of us has had many, many experiences. Through our interaction with the various dynamic factors around us we form and reform, we are illusions constituted in our patterning by ceaseless interaction. None of these specific forms is the real truth or final definition of who we are! I am not a thing, I am a pulsation of responsivity within the field of responsivity, a wave in the ever-shifting pattern of wave movement. Just as we see that the wave is part of the ocean, with wave and ocean integral, so our awareness is intact, not torn, not damaged, not altered. With this we are free of the sickness of effort arising from the false belief that "Something must be done! I will change the situation!"

With clarity we see that we are energy moving with energy, like experiences occurring in a dream. We cannot say it is not happening, because it is experience. Yet it is not real. Real indicates a thing-ness, something existing in and of itself. Nowhere will you find anything which is real. What does occur is a ceaseless display of the diversity of the energy of the ground. Therefore, when you feel the urge to do something, to change something, see this for what it is: an old habit formation. Then relax from the effort of reification and release yourself from your self-identity. Rest in open awareness with subjectivity as energy flowing in the field of energy.

Waves of water are moving in water. However if I think something is wrong, then this judgement freezes the situation. Now these waves of movement are carrying a block of object-ice and in response to this there arises a block of subject-ice. I am consolidated as this person and I'm going to do something! This is the disease of effort. The ice is frozen water. Life is flow, the freezing is death.

The second line concerning the result states: **"Spontaneously abiding and so everything is settled."** Spontaneous indicates that nobody is causing this, neither god, nor the devil, nor the ego. It just is. This is mysterious. It cannot be expressed in language or in conceptual thought for they operate in terms of a subject, a verb and an object. Concepts generate the delusion of entities. This is artifice, contrivance, the perverse make-believe that maintains the delusion of alienation from the ground. No effort is required, for integrity, wholeness, is intrinsic. We simply have to open to the all-inclusive openness. Openness includes all of samsara and nirvana yet remains free of the stain of reification. Thus the energy of the ground can manifest as patterns of identification yet without establishing anything as having inherent existence. Thus the familiar names can be applied to arisings without this being taken to be referring to existent entities.

The energy or potential of the ground manifests diverse patterns. All the patterns that arise are just as they are: settled, perfect, completely themselves. No improvement is required to make some-thing more 'how it is' – how it is, is how it shows. Only under the power of reification do we seek to change what something is. Birds, fish, cows, humans, are patterns of appearance, each with their own sphere of activity as they respond to what occurs for them according to the specificity of their senses and embodiment. Our brief time together will soon come to an end and then we will disperse, each following the trajectories revealed in our co-emergence. Each of us will work with the circumstances we encounter as the shifting templates of our interpretations interact with the sensory field, as it is revealed to us. If you want to get a drink of water, you get up and go to the kitchen. Who is 'you' referring to? Some fixed essence? Your open awareness? This particular patterning of energy? If this was a dharma television quiz program, and you want to win the hundred thousand euros, you have to choose number three. I, who go to the kitchen, am energy flowing to the kitchen. I am going to the kitchen, but nobody is going to the kitchen. Each movement in the progression towards the kitchen is itself complete. If we give an account of what has happened we will totalise myriad discrete moments, each unborn and ungraspable. The totalised version will however offer us the chance to add more concepts and elaborate an even more complex account of what never actually occurred. The actual is always already vanishing.

We manifest as the ever-dynamic radiance of awareness. We are the flow of the energy of awareness. We're not nothing at all, yet we are not something fixed and defined. We are energy participating in the field of the flow of energy. When you look for your own mind to see if it is like the kind of things you know, you won't find it. Your mind, the illuminator of all occurrences is not a thing. It doesn't have a colour or a shape. You can't establish it as big or small, or as inside your body or outside your body. When it arises, we can't find where it came from. When it is present, we're not sure where it is. If it seems to vanish, we don't know where it goes. It is not like any-thing we know. Things have shape and colour and density and so on, but awareness does not. To be settled in and as awareness is not like being settled in a castle on an island where the waves are kept outside. The stillness of awareness and what is arising are not two different arenas. Thus all moments of movement are settled, settled in unchanging awareness.

Liberation is resting in the intrinsic, the always here and now. Ungraspable patterns arise ceaselessly; neither the same nor different, neither one nor many. The primordial purity of the open ground is inseparable from uninterpreted instant presence. The three aspects of unborn openness, unimpeded display and apparitional patterning are inseparable. Unawareness of this is the cause of all the suffering of samsara even though unawareness itself is an illusion. To be aware of the intrinsic is to collapse all the phantoms of delusion. So awakening to the intrinsic is the heart of our practice. It is the function of the Guru Yoga of the white A. Then we rest in openness to the open and are freed from chasing after past events and waiting expectantly for future events.

May we all awaken to our own intrinsic freedom!

Dependent Arising

DEPENDENT ARISING

Dependent arising or dependent origination points to the fact that there are no self-caused or self-existing entities. All phenomena, all experiences, all the possible patterns of occurrence that can ever happen, arise from causes in an interconnectivity which has no beginning or end. At each moment, on the basis of *this* pattern of illusion, *that* pattern of illusion arises. The brief compilation presented here can help us to understand the Four Noble Truths: suffering, the causes of suffering, the ending of suffering, and the path that leads to the ending of suffering. Suffering arises from causes, namely afflictions and actions.

In the Theravada view illustrated in the Wheel of Becoming, the key affliction is ignorance understood as the ongoing ignoring of the absence of inherent existence in people. This ignoring of the ungraspable nature of self and other leads to clinging: clinging to self and clinging to other. Self and other do not exist and yet because these concepts structure our lives we cannot say that they are non-existent. The transient patterns of experience that are claimed to be 'self' have no existence of their own. They arise in dependence on other pattern which, being also empty of 'self', are not truly other either.

Ignorance gives rise to the Three Marks of Conditioned Existence: suffering, impermanence, and the absence of inherent existence. Suffering arises in different forms in each of the six realms. Details can be found in Chapter 1 of *SIMPLY BEING* [1]. The Buddha stated concisely that suffering is getting what you do not want and not getting what you do want. Thus, suffering arises from aversion and desire which ripen from ignorance and mental opacity as represented by the three animals at the centre of the wheel. Suffering in the human realm arises as birth, old age, sickness and death. Once you are born some degree of suffering is inevitable though no one can predict how or when it will occur.

---

[1]

Notes

Refer to Appendix I. Other books by James Low

All that we experience is impermanent: our bodies, our speech, our thoughts, feelings and all mental events. The world around us is impermanent as the seasons change and the climate changes, bringing floods and fires. The changes in politics and economics alter the landscape, and the worlds of our childhood become unrecognisable in what we encounter today. Although we wish to cling on to forms and habits since they give us a sense of reliability, we find that they are not actually stable and that they change due to their dependence on other factors, which are also changing.

The absence of inherent existence in people is indicated by the fact that what we take to be someone is a varying dynamic construct. Traditionally this is described as the five heaps or *skandhas*, the basic constituents which combine and cooperate in diverse ways to generate our perception of people, including ourselves. The five are: form, indicating shape and colour; feeling, indicating positive, neutral or negative responses; perception, indicating the identification of objects via the senses; composition, indicating the incorporation of perceptions into schemas of identification; and consciousness, indicating the organisation of composites according to the use of interpretive concepts. Since all human beings arise in dependence and have no singular core or essence, we can see that they are forms, organised according to 'names'.

The fourth link or *nidana* is illustrated by an image of five men in a boat, i.e. the five constituents. Sometimes only two men are shown in which case the boat is form and the passengers are 'name', or the activation of the form, i.e. the activity of feeling, perception, composition and consciousness. The fact that there are several people in the boat points to the way in which our body, voice and mind develop in relation to those of others. Parents, the wider family, and school are all actively engaging with the young person to elicit their potential and guide it into the pathways privileged by their particular culture.

I am because you are; and how you are with me influences how I can be with you. All humans are mutually conditioning since we are interdependent. Our lives are dynamic, not static. We may think of ourselves as being a separate person, an autonomous unit, isolated from others when we withdraw into ourselves. But this is a delusion. The idea of an enduring self that underpins my sense of being a continuous being, an existent, is based on imagining an entity. The entity of 'self' is an idea, a belief, a make-believe.

The Wheel of Becoming shows the dynamic interactive nature of our life. We are always already part of the field of emergence. Our separate self is a delusion which takes us out of alignment with how life is. Imagining that we are fundamentally apart from what is going on and that we can therefore choose to participate or not is a belief based on ignorance. The experience of isolation arises from ignoring all the evidence that we emerge from our mother, who is already in this world. We emerge into this world as part of it – breathing, drinking and urinating, eating and defecating. We are a flow within the flow. To ignore this, to be unaware of it, to not be awake to it, is the source of all our suffering.

Moreover, according to the mahayana view, the seeming reality of phenomena is a mere name, an attribution, a sign. They are devoid of inherent existence and arise dependently. The actuality of phenomena is signless, empty, and devoid of intention as verses 4-7 on page 93 make clear.

Reified phenomena arise for us due to ignoring the fact that they are actually ungraspable. Ignoring the actual gives rise to imagining all the pseudo-entities refracted through the deluding prism of duality. Belief that these imagined entities are real and can be organised to increase our pleasure and diminish our pain keeps us striving in the Wheel of Becoming. The wheel turns and we run after mirage-like entities only to be disappointed. On and on we go chasing illusions which we believe to be real.

From the Buddhist point of view the whole of samsara, all of conditioned existence, is a prison. Some areas of the prison seem to offer freedom, yet this is a delusion. Even in the god realms, where sensuous pleasure is always available and gross suffering only arises in the final week as we prepare to leave, we are not free of the invisible prison of unawareness. In all the six realms, whether experience is subtle or gross, it is organised around two erroneous beliefs: belief in the inherent existence of phenomena and belief in the inherent difference between subject and object and between all the other polarities.

Our own identity, our sense of being who we believe ourselves to be, seems to be a given, something that just is. Yet when we look without prejudice, we see that we have been deluded. No fixed enduring self can be found – not in ourselves and not in others. We arise in dependent origination, and our own deep sense of individual existence is merely an illusory construct held in place by our lack of insight.

The prison of samsara arises from unawareness of the ever-open ground and source of all. This unawareness of our true basis gives rise to the false notion that we exist in and of ourselves. This notion is the prison we cannot detect because we are inured to it. The fundamental prison is the idea of inherent or independent existence. This is, I am, you are – how effortlessly meaningful these untrue statements are for us. From the initial 'this is', the fact of 'something', all else arises. Facts are made by belief – not to see this is to believe that facts rest on existents. This delusion gives rise to duality, to the mutually excluding definitions which establish the variety of things.

Thus all that we take for granted, all that we believe to be real and reliable, is in fact contrived, compounded, put together by mental activity acting on the concepts generated by mental activity. Reification both freezes the open field of co-emergent becoming and then fragments it into the many things that we seem to encounter, including ourselves. Yet nothing has actually come into true existence. All appearances are unborn; they are illusions fabricated into the erroneous form of self-existing entities. All this is the work of dualistic consciousness desperately seeking to stabilise the flow of interactive experience. Consciousness grasps at ideas and takes them to be substantial objects. This generates our familiar sense of the world. These entities which seemed to validate our existence are actually the mind-forged blinkers that blind us to the open ground of all experience.

The things which constitute our reified experience are then further defined by naming, by the allocation of identificatory signs. Relying on the sign-web of language, each seemingly autonomous subject is able to refine its sense of liking or not liking, friend or foe, adopting or rejecting. Then, believing in the separate reality of self and other, we find ourselves shaped by different intentions: to help, to harm, to win, to collaborate. Acting on the basis of these we generate the karmic fuel which keeps the Wheel of Becoming turning and the inhabitants of samsara always active in trying to optimise pleasure and minimise pain.

So many diverse forms of prison arise from this and so many diverse experiences of being imprisoned. Sentient beings can be imprisoned by wealth and by poverty, by beauty and by plainness, by their own opinions and by others' opinions. Animals live in fear of predators within the food chain and in fear of human jailers who pluck them from the sea, shoot them in the sky and trap them in fields and intense factory farming. For humans they are a means to an end as human concerns are placed first – how many humans would want to ban insecticides for the harm they cause to insects? No, it is all about us.

Yet many humans are also trapped. For example, in dictatorships, in military regimes where the rights of ordinary citizens are disregarded and cruel punishments can be administered without fear of reprisal. To have power over others, to enforce their compliance through fear-inducing threats and control of all resources, brings joy to a few and misery to many. Once the power of the state is directed towards the benefit of a self-selected minority sealed in complacency, the intensity of suffering for the rest makes insight into the fundamental structure especially difficult to achieve.

We can make use of the teachings on dependent arising to see the absence of separate or inherent existence in any appearance, activity, or experience. If we see this we stop ignoring the actual emptiness of phenomena and when the resulting clarity is bright the urge to cling to self and other fades away. With nothing to cling to, the tension of grasping relaxes and we are free to work with the ceaseless play of unborn circumstances.

In all the Dharma traditions, there is an emphasis on wisdom and compassion for together they form the key that unlocks the prison of egotism and brings access to the intrinsic freedom of the mind. May all beings awaken from the nightmares of delusions and be freed from the power of the five poisons. The pure, the good, the inclusive, the welcoming, is intrinsic and has never actually been lost. May we abandon futile striving and relax into the ease offered by our ever-open source. This ease is the basis of effortless inclusive kindness that abandons not a single sentient being and sees them all as the radiance of the Buddha's heart.

If you wish to study this further, you can read the first section of THIS IS IT [2] entitled, *One Thing Leads to Another.*

---

[2] Refer to Appendix I. Other books by James Low

THE MAHAYANA SUTRA ON DEPENDENT ARISING
ARYAPRATITYASAMUTPADANAMAMAHAYANASUTRA

Homage to all Buddhas and Bodhisattvas.

Thus did I hear at one time. The Blessed One was in the Realm of the Thirty-three Gods, seated on the throne of Indra. With him were great hearers such as the venerable Asvajit; bodhisattva mahasattvas such as noble Maitreya, noble Avalokitesvara and Vajrapani, adorned with immeasurable precious qualities; along with various gods such as the great Brahma, lord of the Saha world; and Narayana and Mahesvara; and Sakra, the chief of the gods, and Pancasikha, the king of the gandharvas.

On that occasion, the bodhisattva mahasattva Avalokitesvara rose from his seat, draped his upper robe over one shoulder and knelt down with his right knee on the peak of Mount Meru. With his palms together he bowed to the Blessed One and addressed him with these words:

> "Blessed one, these gods all wish to build a stupa. Now that they are present with us, please teach them the Dharma in such a way that their merit of Brahma will increase and the merit of the monks, nuns, laymen and laywomen will increase more than that of all types of beings in the worlds of gods, maras, Brahma, renunciates and brahmins."

At this, the Blessed One spoke the verse of dependent arising:

ye dharma hetuprabhava
hetum tesam tathagato hy avadat
tesam ca yo nirodha
evamvadi maha sramanah

"Phenomena, whatever they are that arise from causes,
Have their causes and whatever stops them
Taught by the Tathagata.
This has been stated by the great renunciate.

"Avalokitesvara, it is like this. This dependent arising is the dharmakaya of all the Tathagatas. A person who sees dependent arising sees the Tathagata. Avalokitesvara, if a faithful son or daughter of a noble family, in a remote place, builds a stupa the size of a gooseberry fruit, with a central pole the

size of a needle and a parasol the size of a flower of the bakula tree, and inserts this verse of dependent arising which is the dharmadhatu, he or she will generate the merit of Brahma. When such people die they will be reborn in the world of Brahma."

After the Blessed One had spoken, the hearers, bodhisattvas, and the whole assembly, along with the universe of gods, humans, asuras and gandharvas rejoiced and praised his words.

THE MAHAYANA SUTRA ON DEPENDENT ARISING is concluded.

THE TWELVE NIDANA LINKS

In the centre of the wheel of life is a circle coloured blue-black or white, the symbol of the *alayavijnana (Skt.)*, the ground consciousness that is the basis of all that occurs in and as samsara. Within it, chasing each other in a never-ending round of aroused activity, are a black pig, symbol of stupidity; a multicoloured poisonous snake, symbol of anger; and a red and multihued rooster, symbol of desire.

Surrounding the central circle, the six segments representing the six realms are as follows. Starting at the top the syllable in the first segment represents the realm of the gods. Then in clockwise direction, the syllable in the second segment represents the realm of the asuras or jealous gods. The syllable in the third segment represents the realm of the pretas or hungry ghosts. The syllable in the fourth segment represents the realm of the hell beings. The syllable in the fifth segment represents the realm of the animals. The syllable in the sixth segment represents the realm of human beings.

These six realms are surrounded by an outer circle containing the symbols of the twelve links of dependent origination. They are each described on the following three pages.

1) The link of ignorance

Ignorance, the first link, is both the ignoring of what is actually the case and the ignorance of actively imagining that which is not the case. It is illustrated by a blind old person who is unable to find their way.

2) The link of volitional factors/impulses

The second link of volitional formation is illustrated by a potter at his wheel. The pots symbolise the deeds being performed that will mould the future experience of the one who performs them, generating for 'them' a specific life in one of the six realms.

3) The link of consciousness

Consciousness, the third link, is depicted by a monkey swinging from branch to branch in a tree. In a similar manner the consciousness of beings dulled by ignorance springs uncontrollably from object to object.

4) The link of name and form

Name and form, the fourth link, is shown by five people in a boat carried on the stream of becoming. The five people represent the five skandha constituents, form and the four 'names': sensation, perception, composition and consciousness.

5) The link of six sense bases

The six sense-bases, the fifth link, are symbolised by a house with five windows and a door. This illustrates the six sense entrances by which the world is perceived.

6) The link of contact

Contact, the sixth link, is shown by a man and woman embracing.

7) The link of feeling

Feeling, the seventh link, has the picture of the man with an arrow in his eye. This indicates how sense contact has an impact on the subject.

8) The link of craving

Craving, the eighth link, is shown by a woman offering a drink to a man. This illustrates how a pleasant situation will bring with it the desire for its continuation.

9) The link of clinging

Clinging, the ninth link, is the longing to keep that which is desired. This clinging and grasping is the result of previous entanglement and is represented by a man plucking fruit from a tree. It is the urge to hold onto what one believes one has.

10) The link of becoming

Becoming, the tenth link, is represented by a pregnant woman. This indicates a potential which has been awakened but has not yet manifested.

11) The link of birth

Birth, the eleventh link, is shown by a woman giving birth to a child. This indicates the experience of finding oneself separated off as an individual who now has to find thier own way.

12) The link of old age and death

Old-age and death, the twelfth link, is the inevitable end of all episodes of worldly existence. It is shown by people carrying a bier on which a swathed corpse lies in a foetal posture. The one who has died is already moving towards their next birth and the experience of further misery in one of the six realms.

THE HEART OF DEPENDENT ORIGINATION

VERSE AND COMMENTARY

Homage to Manjusri, the ever-youthful

1. The twelve different links,
   Those taught by the Buddha as dependently arising,
   Are fully encompassed by these three,
   Afflictions, actions and suffering.

2. The first,
   1) The link of ignorance

   eighth
   8) The link of craving

   and ninth
   9) The link of clinging

   are afflictions,

   The second
   2) The link of volitional factors/impulses

   and tenth
   10) The link of becoming

   are actions,

92

The remaining seven are suffering.

3) The link of consciousness

4) The link of name and form

5) The link of six sense bases

6) The link of contact

7) The link of feeling

11) The link of birth

12) The link of old age and death

Thus the twelve links are encompassed by these three (afflictions, actions and suffering).

1) The link of ignorance

8) The link of craving

9) The link of clinging

3. From the three

2) The link of volitional factors/impulses

10) The link of becoming

the two

arise.

From the two

2) The link of volitional factors/impulses

10) The link of becoming

the seven arise

3) The link of consciousness

4) The link of name and form

5) The link of six sense bases

6) The link of contact

7) The link of feeling

11) The link of birth

12) The link of old age and death

Moreover from these seven

3) The link of consciousness

4) The link of name and form

5) The link of six sense bases

6) The link of contact

7) The link of feeling

11) The link of birth

12) The link of old age and death

1) The link of ignorance   8) The link of craving   9) The link of clinging

the three arise.

The wheel of life revolves again and again.

4. Since all beings are cause and consequence
   In this way there are no sentient beings at all.
   Phenomena are empty, that is all,
   And from them arise only empty phenomena.

5. As with instructive speech, butter lamps, mirrors, seals,
   Magnifying crystals, seeds, sourness and sound,
   The wise know that although the aggregates emerge in the next life
   They are not transmigrating.

6. Those who impute traceless obliteration
   To the most subtle entities,
   Will, due to their lack of knowledge,
   Not see how they are dependently arisen.

7. In this way there is not the least aspect to be cleared away,
   Nor the slightest aspect to be put in place.
   Truly looking at the actual truth,
   By truly seeing there is complete liberation.

These are the verses on THE HEART OF DEPENDENT ORIGINATION written
by the teacher Arya Nagarjuna.

THE COMMENTARY

The virtuous student who wishes to learn, who is able to listen, retain and recall, and who has the power to clear away discursive thought, approaches close to the teacher and requests instruction in the following manner: 'Regarding the Buddha, "The twelve different links, those taught by the Buddha as dependently arising³", I request that I may study all that is included in this view.' The teacher, having understood this request concerning the specificity of just this aspect of Dharma, replied that they "are fully encompassed in these three, afflictions, actions and suffering." He spoke these words which brought complete clarity.

Regarding this, ten plus two makes twelve. These links are actually different, being different in the manner of the parts that constitute a wooden chariot. This is how they are shown to be linked aspects. The Buddha, the Capable One, is capable in body, voice and mind. What has been spoken by the Buddha should be known as equivalent to demonstration and elucidation. Dependent arising does not come from causes such as inherent existence, fixed essence, reliance on others, gods, time, the real, willpower, or specific location.

These twelve different links rest on the afflictions, actions and suffering which support each other in the manner of the beams of a house. All are fully encompassed in these three. 'Fully' means without exception.

Another question is posed. 'Which of these different links are encompassed within each of the following, afflictions, actions and suffering?' The reply comes,

"The first, eighth and ninth are afflictions."

1) The link of ignorance	8) The link of craving	9) The link of clinging

---

³ Dependent origination and dependent arising are both valid translations and both are used in this text. Experiences arise, appear, emerge from, and have their origin in, other experiences.

The first of these twelve links is ignorance. The eighth is craving. The ninth is clinging. These three are known as afflictions.

If one asks about activity[4],

"The second and the tenth are activity."

2) The link of volitional factors/impulses

10) The link of becoming

The second is volitional formation. The tenth is becoming. These two aspects are known to be encompassed by activity.

"The seven remaining are suffering."

3) The link of consciousness

4) The link of name and form

5) The link of six sense bases

6) The link of contact

7) The link of feeling

11) The link of birth

12) The link of old age and death

The links that remain after the portions allocated to afflictions and activity are the seven links which are known to be suffering. Thus there is consciousness, name and form, the six sense bases, contact, feeling, birth, and old age and death. Moreover this sound (of the word

---

[4] This activity is the karmic activity which acts as a cause having consequences that manifest later.

'suffering') encompasses the sufferings of being separated from what is loved, not being separated from what is not loved, and unfulfilled desires. *"Thus the twelve links are encompassed by these three."*

Therefore these twelve links are known as afflictions, actions and suffering. The Tibetan particle *'Ni'*[5] indicates that there is something further to be stated and the aspects taught in the sutras are now fully completed. Thus it is clear that there are no other factors apart from the links which are shown here.

A question*: 'What specifically gives rise to afflictions, to activity and to suffering? I request you to please explain this.'*

The reply: *"From the three*

1) The link of ignorance   8) The link of craving   9) The link of clinging

the two arise."

2) The link of volitional   10) The link of becoming
     factors/impulses

From the three (ignorance, craving and clinging), which are known as the afflictions, arise the two (volitional formation and becoming), which are known as activity.

---

[5] The 'Ni' is placed in the line between "the twelve links" and "are encompassed by these three". This indicates their equivalence.

"From the two

2) The link of volitional
factors/impulses

10) The link of becoming

the seven arise."

3) The link of
consciousness

4) The link of name
and form

5) The link of six
sense bases

6) The link of contact

7) The link of feeling

11) The link of birth

12) The link of old age
and death

These are the seven indicated above (consciousness, name and form, the six sense bases, contact, feeling, birth, and old age and death) which are known as suffering.

"Moreover from these seven the three arise" that are known as the afflictions.

1) The link of ignorance

8) The link of craving

9) The link of clinging

"Furthermore, from these three afflictions the two arise."

2) The link of volitional factors/impulses

10) The link of becoming

Thus, *"The wheel of life revolves again and again."*

There are three modes (or realms) of life (or becoming), desire, form and formless within which the wheel revolves without coming to rest. Due to this beings wander everywhere in the world. The Tibetan particle 'Ni' (placed between 'the wheel' and 'ceaselessly revolving') indicates a sense of uncertainty. The precious wheel turns (in a regular fashion) but the (revolving wheel of) becoming in these three (realms) does not occur in that way. Hence uncertainty is indicated.

A question: *'Now, who made sentient beings? Was it the lord of all that is embodied? How was this work done?'*

The reply: *"Since all beings are cause and consequence, in this way,"* except by attribution[6] *"there are no sentient beings at all."* If we truly examine this[7] we see that even the attribution does not exist. It is not fitting that what is merely an attribution should be adhered to as a real object.

A question: *'If this is so, then who passes from this world to the next?'*

The reply: From this world to the next not even an atom of dust transmigrates. Moreover, *"Phenomena are empty, that is all, and from them arise only empty phenomena."* Phenomena are without a self and what pertains to a self. What are known as afflictions and actions have become causes. From these five links (*afflictions:* ignorance, craving, clinging; *actions:* volitional formation and becoming), which are empty, come the consequent result of what is called suffering (which is also)

---

[6] brTag-Pa, examining and investigating on the basis of identification through signs. This indicates attributing an 'essence' by the act of naming, installing a superimposed identity which is not inherent.

[7] That which seems to exist on the basis of believing the attribution (including the attribution itself).

free of self and what pertains to self. Thus there are deemed to arise the described (attributed) seven empty phenomena (factors, links) (*suffering:* consciousness, name and form, the six sense bases, contact, feeling, birth, and old age and death).

Regarding what is thus stated, all that follows on from what is without self or that which pertains to self is never self or that which pertains to self. Moreover from phenomena (factors, links), which are inherently without self, arise only phenomena which are inherently without self. This should be understood just as it has been explained.

A question: *'What examples illustrate how only phenomena without inherent self (existence) arise from phenomena without an inherent self?'*

The reply: *"As with instructive speech, butter lamps, mirrors, seals, magnifying crystals, seeds, sourness and sound."* By enquiring using these examples one can know the inherent absence of self (existence) as well as subsequent manifestation in the world. For example, if the words from the teacher's mouth were (fully) transferred to the student then the teacher would be deprived of her own words. Hence there is no transference. Nor does the reply of the student arise from something other otherwise there would be no cause. In this way, as with the speech from the teacher's mouth, so with the mind at the time of death. It does not travel across to the next life otherwise there would be the fault of permanence. Nor does the next life arise from something other otherwise there would be the fault of being without cause. Hence, it is impossible to say if what arises from the cause of the teacher's speech arises identically or not for the student. Similarly it is impossible to say if the mind at the point of death and the mind assigned to the arising birth are identical or different.

In like manner, with (the flame) of one butterlamp another lamp is lit. And from a face the mirror shows a reflection; from a seal an impression; from a magnifying crystal a fire; from a seed a shoot; with the juice of sour fruit saliva arises; and from a sound an echo arises. With these examples (one can see that) it is not possible to know if what arises is the same or different.

Hence, *"The wise know that although the aggregates emerge in the next life they are not transmigrating."* There are five aggregates[8]: form, feeling, perception/apprehension, volitional formation and consciousness/comprehending. Their emerging in another life indicates that from a cause that has stopped another consequence/result arises. Yet not even an atom's worth of substantial entity has transmigrated from this world to the next. Because it is like this, the revolving wheel (of life) arises due to the subtle propensity for erroneous thought. The humble Tibetan particle *'Yang'* (even, yet) indicates opposition, a rejection[9]. (If one sees that) all entities are impermanent, suffering and empty, and are always insubstantial (then one) will not be deluded concerning entities.

Free of delusion/stupefaction there is no attachment. With no attachment aversion does not occur. With no aversion actions will not be performed. With no actions there is no adopting of/involvement in entities. With no involvement there is no construction of becoming. With no becoming there is no birth. If there is no birth, suffering of body and mind will not arise. In this way, as shown here, if the five causes (aggregates) are not engaged with then no other result will arise. With this the end is known. In this way the wrong views of permanence and annihilation are dispelled. There are two stanzas which address this:

Those who impute traceless obliteration
To the most subtle entities,
Will, due to their lack of knowledge,

---

[8] Delusion gives rise to the first aggregate, the sense of form as substance and thereby generates seemingly separate objects. Towards such objects the second aggregate, feelings arise and they can be positive, negative or neutral, and this encourages discrimination and choice. This leads to the third aggregate, apprehension by which specific objects are taken hold of as being of particular interest. With this there is the fourth aggregate, volitional formation that manifests as an urge to get involved, to do something to someone or something. From this there arises the fifth and final aggregate, consciousness, which is our capacity to comprehend a situation according to our own conceptual capacity.

[9] Of the idea of the continuity of the aggregates, and hence there is the possibility of the reversal of the twelve links.

Not see how they are dependently arisen.

In this way there is not the least aspect to be cleared away,
Nor the slightest aspect to be put in place.
Truly looking at the actual truth,
By truly seeing there is complete liberation.

This completes the explanation of THE HEART OF DEPENDENT ARISING
written by Acharya Arya Nagarjuna.

གང་གི་རྟེན་ཅིང་འབྲེལ་པར་འབྱུང་།

GANG	GI	TEN CHING	DREL WAR	JUNG
whatever	*of*	*depending*	*connected*	*arise*

Whatever arises through dependent connection is

འགགས་པ་མེད་པ་སྐྱེད་མེད་པ།

GAG PA	ME PA	KYE	ME PA
stopping,	*without*	*arising,*	*without*
ceasing		*born*	

Without ceasing or arising,

ཆད་པ་མེད་པ་རྟག་མེད་པ།

CHE PA	ME PA	TAG	ME PA
annihilated,	*without*	*permanent,*	*without*
cut off		*eternal*	

Without annihilation or permanence,

འོང་བ་མེད་པ་འགྲོ་མེད་པ།

ONG WA	ME PA	DRO	ME PA
coming	*without*	*going*	*without*

Without coming or going,

ཐ་དད་དོན་མིན་དོན་གཅིག་མིན།

THA DAE	DON	MIN	DON	CHI	MIN
different	*meaning*	*without*	*meaning*	*same*	*without*

Without difference or sameness.

སྤྲོས་པ་ཉེར་ཞི་ཞི་བསྟན་པ།

TRO PA	NYER	ZHI	ZHI	TAN PA
thought	*fully*	*pacifying*	*peaceful*	*doctrine,*
proliferation				*teaching*

This peaceful teaching that stills dualistic thought

རྫོགས་པའི་སངས་རྒྱས་སྨྲ་རྣམས་ཀྱི།

DZOG PAI **SANG GYE** **MA NAM** **KYI**
complete, *Buddha* *teaching,* *of*
perfect *speaking*

Is the holy teaching of the perfect Buddha.

དམ་པ་དེ་ལ་ཕྱག་འཚལ་ལོ།།

DAM PA **DE** **LA** **CHA TSHAL LO**
holy, best *that* *to* *bow down, salute*

I bow in reverence to this.

Whatever arises through dependent connection is without ceasing or arising, without annihilation or permanence, without coming or going, without difference or sameness. This peaceful teaching that stills dualistic thought is the holy teaching of the perfect Buddha. I bow in reverence to this.

Arya Nagarjuna, from his ROOT VERSES OF THE MIDDLE WAY

DEDICATION

ཨྱཱུཿ དགེ་དང་མི་དགེའི་རྟོག་ཚོགས་རང་གྲོལ་ལཿ

Aa	GE	DANG	MI GEI	TOG	TSO	RANG DROL	LA
	virtuous	*and*	*unvirtuous*	*thoughts*	*all*	*self-liberating*	*with*

Aa With all virtuous and non-virtuous thoughts being self-liberating, and

རེ་དང་དོགས་པའི་མཚན་མ་མི་དམིགས་ཀྱང་ཿ

RE	DANG	DO PAI	TSEN MA	MI	MIG	KYANG
hopes	*and*	*doubts*	*signs,*	*not*	*take that object*	*also,*
			characteristics		*conceptualise*	*although*

Being free of identifying with the signs that generate hopes and fears,

སྣང་ཆའི་རྟེན་འབྲེལ་བསླུ་མེད་དགེ་ཚོགས་རྒྱུནཿ

NANG CHAI	TEN DREL	LU ME	GE	TSO	GYUN
appearances,	*connection,*	*not cheating*	*virtue*	*collection*	*always flow*
ideas	*(relative truth*				
	absence of inherent existence)				

The accumulation of virtue keeps flowing from the undeceiving dependent origination of appearances.

ཟག་མེད་ཆོས་ཀྱི་དབྱིངས་སུ་བསྔོ་བར་བྱཿ

ZAG ME	CHOE KYI YING	SU	NGO WAR	JA
pure,	*all encompassing*	*in*	*give,*	*do*
undefiled	*space*		*dedicate*	

This is dedicated in undefiled all-encompassing space for the benefit of all beings.

Aa With all virtuous and non-virtuous thoughts being self-liberating, and being free of identifying with the signs that generate hopes and fears, the accumulation of virtue keeps flowing from the undeceiving dependent origination of appearances. This is dedicated in undefiled all-encompassing space for the benefit of all beings.

DHARMA ADVICE

ཆོས་རྣམས་ཐམས་ཅད་རྒྱུ་ལས་བྱུང་།

CHOE NAM   **TAM CHE**   **GYU**   **LAE**   **JUNG**
phenomena,   *all*   *cause*   *from*   *arise*
appearances
All phenomena arise from a cause.

དེ་རྒྱུ་དེ་བཞིན་གཤེགས་པས་གསུངས།

DE   **GYU**   **DE ZHIN SHE PE**   **SUNG**
that   *cause*   *Tathagata, Buddha, by*   *spoken, told*
This cause has been shown by the Tathagata.

རྒྱུ་ལ་འགོག་པ་གང་ཡིན་པ།

GYU   **LA**   **GO PA**   **GANG**   **YIN PA**
cause   *from*   *stop*   *whatever*   *is*
How to put an end to this cause

དགེ་སྦྱོང་ཆེན་པོས་འདི་སྐད་གསུངས།

GE   **JONG**   **CHEN POE**   **DI**   **KE**   **SUNG**
virtue   *practitioner*   *great by*   *that*   *speech*   *said*
Has been taught by the great practitioner of virtue

All phenomena arise from a cause. This cause has been shown by the Tathagata. How to put an end to this cause has been taught by the great practitioner of virtue.

སྡིག་པ་ཅི་ཡང་མི་བྱ་ཞིང་།

DIG PA   **CHI YANG**   **MI**   **JA ZHING**
sin   *whatsoever*   *not*   *doing*
Not to do anything unvirtuous whatsoever but

དགེ་བ་ཕུན་སུམ་ཚོགས་པར་སྤྱད།

GE WA   **PHUN SUM TSOG PAR**   **JAE**
virtue   *all good things, good ideas*   *do*
To practise virtue and all that is good and

རང་གི་སེམས་ནི་ཡོངས་སུ་འདུལ།

RANG GI SEM NI   YONG SU   DUL
own mind   fully   control
To fully control one's own mind –

འདི་ནི་སངས་རྒྱས་བསྟན་པ་ཡིན།

DI NI   SANG GYE   TEN PA   YIN
this is   Buddha's   doctrine   is
This is the doctrine of the Buddha.

Not to do anything unvirtuous whatsoever but to practise virtue and all that is good and to fully control one's own mind – this is the doctrine of the Buddha

Awakening to Emptiness
The Heart Sutra

AN OVERVIEW

We are going to look at the *THE HEART SUTRA*, a very important text in the development of buddhism. We will look at it in terms of both the view or philosophy and the reflective practice. *THE HEART SUTRA* is concerned with deconstructing our basic assumptions about who we are and the nature of the world we live in.

The sutra offers a means to understand how our own mental processes create ways of interpreting and seeing which unfortunately also create a kind of dull clarity. Our usual way of seeing appears to offer clarity because it gives us a sense of knowing something. Yet it is also dull because this way of using knowledge about reified entities is itself a kind of veil or screen which prevents us seeing directly how we actually are and how the world is.

Our minds are both very bright and very lazy. When you spend time with small children you can see how shining their minds are. With great curiosity they are looking and touching, putting things in their mouth and exploring what each item is. Gradually however they accumulate knowledge about how things are and how the people around them are. Knowing the names and functions of the objects in their world, their minds start running ahead of their embodied presence. Because they think they know what is there, they no longer look with curiosity. They are becoming blinded by their own assumptions. You can see children walking to school with big bags on their backs filled with lots of books. Their body has been turned into a donkey – a donkey in the service of a mind that is dedicated to the task of accumulating information.

Buddhist teaching highlights that the mind is chief, the maker of all things. Mind here refers not just to the cognitive function but to the fundamental capacity to be aware, which is the source and ground of all experience. The body and the senses – smell, taste, touch and so on – are each and all the energy or display of the mind. It is not that there is a real division between the mind and the body; they are not different domains. Rather our mind is the luminous clarity which reveals both what we take to be 'myself' and what we take to be 'other'. This luminous clarity is not an observer, not something standing apart from experience but is illumination non-dual with experience. Thus the 'I', which is our open awareness and the 'I', which is our self-referential ego, are not two different things or states. The self-referential ego is how the illuminating energy of awareness appears when it is taken to be 'something', an entity apart from its source. The openness of awareness is itself the basis from which, and in which, the energy or movement of manifestation occurs. It is not something personal that is sealed off from other people and our environment, since all that occurs is equal in its status of being aspects of our experience.

There is no fundamental difference between self and other. However, our sense of our body as something that moves through space and time creates for us the sense that we exist as something apart from everything else. When we look it is obvious that our self is always changing in terms of the thoughts, feelings, and memories and so on that constitute it, yet we still believe that we exist as a continuous reliably present 'me'. We know that we can get up and walk through the room and this freedom of movement seems to be a sign of our separation from the environment. When I get up and move around, it is as if the whole of me is moving. But when I walk outside, I see the mist, and the mist makes me think of the loss of the summer. My body may be in autumn, but my mind is thinking 'summer'. With this there is not just a separation of self and world but also of my body and my mind. Not only am I thinking about the summer but different memories arise, some sweet, some bitter. With the sweet memory, I relax and open. With the bitter memory, I retract and close down. So now I feel that I have a body and a mind and my mind is split into bitter and sweet memories. Some of the sweet memories were moments of being lost in something. Noticing this I might even become suspicious of my sweet memories. Moreover, some of the bitter memories have been useful since they led me to learn something. So the sweet memories become bitter because I got lost, and the bitter memories become sweet because I learned something. Truly we are complicated creatures! Recognising this we feel we have to try to make sense of our life, even though it involves a lot of mental and emotional energy.

The practice of meditation offers us a different possibility of seeing how we are since it focuses on releasing our preoccupation and involvement with our fluctuating mental activity. All that we experience, including all that we take to be 'ourselves', is changing. We cannot find any fixed reliable substantial entities. This actual absence condemns us to chase after the idea of substantial entities again and again. As a relief from this, meditation allows us to be present with the arising and passing of phenomena. It helps us to see what is occurring more clearly than before and with less investment and identification. Meditation awakens us to a freshness of experience that reveals the freshness of the world and the freshness of our awareness.

Meditation is not about arriving at a safe place where you can fall asleep in your assumptions. You arrive at a truly safe place through being awake. This safe place is simply the present moment, the ungraspable experience of being fully present in each moment as it occurs. However this is not a safety that our ego-self appreciates because it means not privileging what we take to be 'good' moments over what we take to be 'bad' moments. Such habitual preference would condemn us to ceaseless judgement and evaluation. Riding on the resultant hopes and fears we would be like a cork on the sea, lifted up and cast down by the movement of the waves of events.

If, however, we can simply be open and present then we can start to see that a shiny moment and a dull moment have the same ground, the same basis. Then we can start to experience equanimity. Rather than being lifted up and happy when life is sweet and cast down and depressed when life is bitter, we relax into the openness which welcomes both the sweet and the bitter as being equally the play of our mind's energy. This is the heart of the practice.

After he gained enlightenment under the bodhi tree in Bodhgaya, Buddha Shakyamuni decided that he wouldn't teach. He reflected that the experience he had had was beyond speech and so how could he talk about it. Even if he said something, people would not understand. He walked up and down a short path beside the bodhi tree for seven days. All the gods came and showered flowers around him and said, "Please, please say something, you have understood the truth." They kept asking and Brahma, the chief of all the gods, made many requests and eventually, out of compassion, the Buddha said, 'Yes'.

The Buddha's decision to teach arose from the tension between his wisdom, which advised not to teach, and his compassion, which called on him to offer whatever was possible. The Buddha taught because of the requests that were made. Without the requests it is likely that he would not have taught since he had no egoic need to impress or convert. The teaching of dharma is relational; it is an aspect of compassion. Wisdom itself cannot be spoken; the teaching of dharma is a flow of compassion that seeks to direct students towards their own intrinsic capacity for wisdom of awakening. Teaching is the energetic connection arising through an ambiance within which the veils of assumption can fall away. The Buddha showed the dharma by his presence. By offering teaching the Buddha related to people's reliance on concepts and this allowed them to gradually open to how he was and to find that openness in themselves.

When you learn to ride a horse, the most important thing is to find your seat, to find a way of sitting on the horse that allows the horse to know that you are with it. Then the horse will feel your relaxation, your warmth, your confidence, and it too will settle. Each person who learns to ride has to find their own seat. The teacher's knowledge of how to sit on a horse is not something that they can give to the student. Each of us has to look, to explore, to taste it for ourselves. This means we have to be willing not to know, to be beginners. We have to avoid the error of applying what we already know to each new situation, for if we do that, fresh new learning will not arise.

Not knowing, however, often makes us feel stupid, and when it comes to seeking wisdom, there is a lot that we have to not know! In particular we have to know how to not know all that we do know. Our existing knowledge is based on reliance on concepts, on an accumulation of facts and reflections. It can be painful to recognise that it is this very knowledge, this reliance on the contents of our mind, which distracts us from the intrinsic clarity of our ever-present awareness.

Each of us knows many things. What we know is like a wonderful face cream, we rub it in and it makes our skin glow. We rub our knowledge into ourselves and it makes our ego feel shiny and competent. But when we find that we have to do some activity we don't understand, our shine vanishes and we feel dull and flat. I remember as a child on Sunday evening, trying to do my homework for Monday morning. I would look at the same pages again and again and not understand anything. Sometimes it would feel very, very difficult and I would end up crying. Then I would go and ask my father:

— Can you help me with this?

—*Yes, it is not so difficult.*

—So if it is not difficult, why don't you just do it for me?

—*Because you have to do it. It is your homework.*

— But how can I do it when I don't know it?

—*Well, that is what you are finding out.*

In these moments it is manifest that learning makes us feel stupid before it makes us shine. If we don't have to learn more, we can feel quite confident. That is why many people don't have any books in their house. You leave school, you don't have to study anymore. Then you can be confident about who you are. But we, the unfortunate ones, have gathered here to learn something new and this is not easy! We need courage, focused attention and patience. We are going to explore how we hide ourselves from ourselves.

The Buddha structured his first teachings around what are referred to as the Four Noble Truths. These are: the fact that there is suffering; the fact that suffering has a cause; the fact that this suffering could come to an end; and the fact that there is a way to bring this suffering to an end. The Buddha pointed out that there are two main kinds of suffering: getting what you don't want and not getting what you do want. A lot of our experience falls within these two categories. Suffering arises because we are attached to our idea of our real existence. We want to be real eternal entities; we want to possess the joy we seek yet these wishes remain unfulfilled.

To be completely present in each moment, as it is unfolding, requires the exquisite timing of a musician or a dancer. Yet we rarely inhabit that fresh presence. Mostly we inhabit the realm of concepts and ideas by which we formulate our notions of ourselves, of the objects of our desire, and of how we could gain them. When we formulate a desire towards something that we want, we evoke a mental image. This mental image then separates off from the context in which it arose and takes on a life of its own. We start to imagine a future orientated towards this image and new ideas arise on the basis of our imagining. So many things are possible as ideas! This freedom to imagine is unobstructed because the future is open. None of us knows what will happen. We don't know how long we will live. We don't know if we will be healthy. We don't know if we will be financially secure or not. We don't know if the people close to us will continue to want to be close to us. The future is yet to unfold. It is fundamentally unknowable no matter what we had planned or hoped for. Due to the intoxication produced by imagining we pay less and less attention to what is actually occurring.

When we develop our plans or imaginings about the future, what they show us is not the future itself but the matrix, the basic frame, out of which we imagine our life. The structure of our hopes and fears shows us our orientation, our bias, our selectivity – a major part of which is our capacity to ignore those factors that cause us distress. If we are not settled in the openness of the present moment, then our thoughts and fantasies about the future appear to refer to something real and knowable. Our own imagination helps us to fabricate maps which bear little resemblance to the actual immediate terrain we encounter.

Working with circumstances means to be present in each moment and be willing to embrace our life as it unfolds for us. We participate, we mobilise our energy and our effort, and this has some influence on what occurs. Yet we cannot achieve the mastery our ego-self seeks because mastery is an illusion. The flow of life is beyond the ego's command. We find ourselves experiencing lack, the sense that something is missing in our life, something that will make us complete. A love story, an enjoyable job, a great place to live – these can all provide some amelioration, some softening of the intensity of the lack, but they cannot remove its root. The root of the lack is our not being settled in ourselves as we actually are. Ignoring our own true nature, we find ourselves alienated.

Our intrinsic openness is always already present here and now, but we look somewhere else. By looking over there we cannot see what is right here.

This is like a person who goes out on the hills looking for their cow when all the time the cow is back home in the barn. We imagine that there is some external object that will fulfil our lives but our ego-self is like a bucket with a hole in it, it is always going to leak no matter how often we fill it up. We like to fall in love, for example, and the feeling this generates is like a big stream of water coming into our bucket. But the hole in the bottom of the bucket is still there. Once the intensity of

116

our feeling starts to decline the amount of water coming into the bucket is no longer greater than the amount of water going out of the bucket. Then we feel sad, "Oh, I don't know what's happened, I used to be so much in love and now I'm beginning to get a bit bored. But there is this new guy at work and he is kind of cute... Maybe he could really fill my bucket..." We can spend our whole life looking for new sources of water, but we are avoiding the actual problem. Having a bucket that leaks as our primary site of identity is not very wise! In fact it is the engine which keeps us wandering in the six realms of samsara. We are restless creatures endlessly seeking completion through gaining impermanent experiences. How very sad!

The path to freeing ourselves from suffering is referred to as the Eightfold Noble Path: right view, right intention, right speech, right action, right livelihood, right effort, right mindfulness and right concentration. By adopting these ways of looking and behaving, we gradually free ourselves from our assumptions. Then we can start to see that our body and voice and mind are each ungraspable. We are not entities and we do not need special entities to complete us. Therefore, rather than trying to find whatever perfect shiny object we currently think we lack, we open ourselves to our awareness of how life actually is, once we stop telling it what it is. The appearance of graspable entities arises from our own deluding mental activity. Believing that there are real objects existing apart from my real self, I grasp at them. The frustration this generates is the root of all suffering everywhere.

Hence true freedom is not a freedom to consume the world and grasp more and more shiny objects. Rather it is the freedom to open one's heart in compassionate ethical relatedness to all that occurs. This is infinite freedom. Each being we meet has their own particular shaping, their own particular qualities, and our freedom to relate to them as they are, simultaneously keeps us free of our habitual tendencies to put ourselves first. To relate to the other as other without pulling them into our own frames of reference requires that we are undefended, free of self-protection and self-interest and thereby free to manifest in whatever way the situation requires. This is very different from thinking, "I will become whatever is necessary to get my bucket filled." Abandoning that centripetal focus our open heart is centrifugal, flowing out into the unfolding field of which we are always already a part. The ego is an accountant, always calculating gain and loss, but awareness is simply open and hospitable.

Intrinsic awareness is not the product of our effort. Our effort, if not ego directed, can help to guide us away from the distraction which keeps us in ignorance of our own awareness. Undistracted presence as awareness is the basis of the three modes or kayas, the ripe presence of a Buddha's enlightenment.

The first is the dharmakaya, the mind of the Buddha – open empty, spacious and devoid of any constitutive content. The sambhogakaya is the radiance of the rich potential of the Buddha's clarity. The nirmanakaya is the illusory way in which the Buddha manifests for the sake of others. The dharmakaya is for ourselves; it is all that we need as it is the ending of lack. The two other form modes (sambhogakaya and nirmanakaya) arise for the sake of others. If we want to achieve profound satisfaction, peace and completion we have to look where this is to be found – we have to open ourselves to our own ever-present true nature. Our nature, the ground of our being, is not dependent on anyone or anything else. Although it has never been lost, it is to be 'found' by being present with oneself. When we rest in our basic openness and the agitation caused by the delusion of the ego-self subsides, then we are complete. This is called dzogchen, the whole, the intrinsic integrity present from the very beginning. Freed from need and grasping, our energy arises effortlessly without the duality of self and other.

The mind is infinite. Thoughts are finite. Feelings are finite. Sensations are finite. When we merge into our thoughts, feelings, sensations, we fuse into the limited, into the small – and so we feel limited and small. This is what is called 'wandering in samsara'. However if that small particular shape is one that is manifesting free of ego-identity in order to connect with a specific situation, then one can be aware that this finite particular shape in this particular moment is inseparable from the infinite openness of the mind within which it moves. This non-duality is the goal of meditation. If, however, the finite shape is taken to be who we are and becomes the site of 'my identity' then in that moment of identification there is forgetfulness of the infinite. The Buddhas' middle way avoids all extremes, so don't fuse into the moment as if it were the total truth, nor try to push the world away and stand apart from it. The finite and the infinite are inherently inseparable.

The flow of experience non-dual with emptiness is unceasing and due to this non-duality it does not establish anything. Everything is like an illusion – to grasp at it is a sign of our delusion. Our posture, our breath, the way we speak, our thoughts and so on are all arising and passing, arising and passing. It is tempting to think that we need to grasp at what occurs and can use it to stabilise our sense of ourselves, but this is delusion. Taking an illusion to be real and substantial, is to be lost, to wander in our imagination, even while life's actuality is here with us and as us all the time.

We believe, think and talk ourselves into existence. We create narratives and stories about who we are. This is an auto-intoxication due to which we fall asleep in the dreamscape of language. The paradox is that the more you can describe your experience, the more you can hide the actuality of your experience.

As soon as we learn to speak, we learn to lie. This is the first real freedom that children experience. Once they understand that they can say that they didn't do something that actually they did do – and that their mother believes them – well, this is something quite momentous!

The gap between how it is and what is said about it establishes a private life, a separation between ourselves and others. It creates our inner world in which I have experience to which you have no direct access. You can only have a mediated access since you are dependent on what I tell you and your own reading of how you take me to be. Now that I am in charge of my story I can choose to add some spice into what I tell you! I can tell you what you want to hear, or I can tell you what you don't want to hear. This generates a sense of control which simultaneously offers freedom and imprisonment: the freedom to manipulate meanings and the prison of the intrapsychic and interpersonal complexity which this generates.

Due to specific causes and circumstances operating in our culture certain propositions appear to be the case. For example, children are often encouraged to get a so-called 'good' job and make a lot of money. Yet the belief that this will bring true value and happiness may well not be true. We believe the proposition because our mind is already tilted towards privileging our own welfare and so is prone to certain distorting factors.

Amongst these are the five poisons: mental dullness, aversion, desire, jealousy and pride. Each of these has many sub-tendencies which inflect our positioning in any situation. When our mind is pervaded by these tendencies it is as if we are looking through distorting glasses. What we then see seems to be the case for we are used to trusting our beliefs and received opinions rather than the actual shape of events.

So what can we trust? The tradition says to trust the tradition, trust the teacher. Can we trust people who say, "Trust me"? Even if we do, some degree of interpretation is necessary since we have to make sense of what the teacher is saying by applying it to our own situation. Starting to examine ourselves, to look at who we are, at how we are, at what we are up to, is not an easy task. Yet it is worthwhile, for the tension between looking for truth and getting lost in illusion can gradually put both activities into question. Lessening our commitment to effortful looking allows space for the actuality of our mind to be revealed.

Simply seeing without interpretation is direct. Trusting is always at one step removed. Trusting takes us toward the abstract, toward whatever concept we believe in, whereas seeing returns us to this specific moment of occurrence. The specific is immediate and impermanent. Concrete moments are unrepeatable. This becomes apparent when you are walking in the mountains. Each step you take brings you a slightly different view. Each moment is always the view from 'here' and each 'here' is changing, just as each 'now' is changing. Our embodied existence is always positioned exactly somewhere at some specific time. We don't have a helicopter to take us up into the sky to see everything. In our abstract thought we may imagine that we have just such an overview, but this is just an idea. Our actuality, the occurrence of our embodied being, is always precise, concrete and already vanishing.

The key point is to see how 'here' is, to see how 'now' is – not to imagine them or to construct them out of our assumptions. This requires us to be present at the site of seeing. Releasing our fixation on interpretation and on linking concepts into narratives, we can relax into our open awareness which is always present and available. When we are open, empty of beliefs, habits and projections, there is space to be with what is there before we think, before we choose, before we act.

Awareness is the ground of our being. With awareness the arising display patterning is self-liberating: without the presence of awareness there is only a landslide of stuff for us to sort out.

THE HEART SUTRA

THE HEART OF PERFECT LIBERATING TRANSCENDENTAL WISE DISCERNING

In the language of India: Bhagawatiprajnaparamitahridaya. In the language of Tibet: bChom-lDan-'Das-Ma Shes-Rab-Kyi Pha-Rol-Tu Phyin-Pa'i sNying-Po. Forming just one bundle of paper.

Thus I have heard: at one time Bhagawan was staying at the Vulture Peak hill at Rajagriha together with a great assembly of the sangha of ordained monks and bodhisattvas.

At that time Bhagawan was resting evenly in the absorbed contemplation known as 'Profound Illumination' which discerns the nature of phenomena.

At that time the great bodhisattva Arya Avalokitesvara was clearly observing within the profound practice of transcendental wise discerning. Through this he truly saw the natural emptiness of the five factors of composition.

Then, through the power of the Buddha, the venerable Shariputra spoke as follows to the Bodhisattva-Mahasattva Arya Avalokitesvara, *"In what manner should they train, those of good family who wish to follow the profound practice of transcendental wise discerning?"* Thus he spoke.

Bodhisattva-Mahasattva Arya Avalokitesvara made this reply to the venerable Shariputra, *"Shariputra, whichever of those sons or daughters of a good family wish to follow the profound practice of transcendental wise discerning should look thoroughly in the manner I will describe and thus clearly see that the five factors of composition are intrinsically empty of inherent self-existence.*

Form is empty. Emptiness is form. Emptiness is not other than form. Form is not other than emptiness. In the same way, feelings, perceptions, formations and consciousness are all empty.

Thus, Shariputra, in that way all phenomena are themselves emptiness. They are free of signs and identification. They are unborn and unceasing, without stain and without freedom from stains, and are without decrease or completion.

Therefore, Shariputra, emptiness is without form, without feeling, without perception, without formation and without consciousness; without eye, without ear, without nose, without tongue, without body, without mentation; without form, without sound, without smell, without taste, without sensation, and without objects of mentation. Emptiness is without the domain of vision and without the domain of the other senses up to and including the domain of mentation. And emptiness is without all the domains of consciousness up to and including mentation consciousness.

Emptiness is free of ignorance, and of the extinction of ignorance and of all twelve factors of dependent co-arising up until old age and death and the extinction of old age and death. Similarly, emptiness is free of suffering, its cause, its cessation and the path that leads to the cessation of suffering. Emptiness is free of intrinsic original knowing and is free of attainment and also of non-attainment.

Therefore Shariputra, because there is nothing to be gained, bodhisattvas rely on transcendental wise discerning and, dwelling with minds free of obscuration, are without fear. Having passed completely from the domain of deception they attain the full release of nirvana.

All buddhas abiding in the three times also rely on transcendental wise discerning and thus, with unexcelled, perfect awakening, are completely enlightened buddhas.

Due to this being so, *"This is the mantra of transcendental wise discerning, the mantra of great awareness, the unsurpassed mantra. This is the mantra which balances the unbalanced. This is the mantra which completely purifies all suffering. This is not deception so you can come to know that it is true.*

Recite the mantra of transcendental wise discerning:

*TADYATHA OM GATE GATE PARAGATE PARASAMGATE
BODHI SVAHA*

In this way, gone, gone, gone beyond, fully gone beyond.

Awakened – as it is!

Shariputra, in this way a Bodhisattva-Mahasattva should train in profound transcendental wise discerning."

Then Bhagawan arose from his absorbed contemplation and praised the Bodhisattva-Mahasattva Arya Avalokitesvara, saying, *"Very good. Very good. Son of a good family, it is like that. It is like that, and so profound transcendental wise discerning is to be practised just as you have shown it. All the Tathagatas will rejoice at this."*

Bhagawan spoke thus, and then the venerable Shariputra and the bodhisattva Avalokitesvara and all of their retinues, and all the gods, men, jealous gods, local spirits and so on of the world rejoiced and sincerely praised the speech of the Bhagawan Buddha.

This concludes 'THE HEART OF PERFECT LIBERATING
TRANSCENDENTAL WISE DISCERNING'.

COMMENTARY

THE HEART SUTRA is a critique of our assumptions about identity. Its title in Sanskrit is *BHAGAVATI PRAJNAPARAMITA HRIDAYA*. In Tibetan this is *bCom lDan 'Das Ma Shes Rab Kyi Pha Rol Tu Phyin Pa'I sNying Po* which means *THE HEART OF PERFECT LIBERATING TRANSCENDENTAL WISE DISCERNING.*

What kind of discerning wisdom is this? It is the one which takes you to the other side. That is to say, it goes beyond our usual knowledge, which is knowledge of things. It is a discernment which sees the illusory nature of seemingly self-existing entities.

Traditional images for this illusory nature are a mirage or a rainbow or an echo. In the summertime when you drive along the road and it is hot, you start to see water shimmering in front of you. There is no water there. This is an optical illusion created by the quality of the air and the heat. When we see a rainbow in the sky something similar is occurring. We can say something is there because we see it. Yet there is no essence to a rainbow; is has no existence of its own. We can't catch it. It arises due to the angle of the sun and refractive index of the tiny droplets of rain which form the cloud. Due to causes and conditions the rainbow briefly occurs. Key amongst these causes and conditions is our capacity to see and conceptualise rainbows. There is no essence of rainbow giving rise to the rainbow; it is an appearance generated by factors outside itself. It has no substance of its own. Transcendent wisdom is wisdom without substantial essence which shows the absence of essence in everything. It is the wisdom of emptiness revealed to us when we don't get taken in by our own constructions.

The sutra begins, **Thus have I heard**. It is said that the Buddha's main disciple, Ananda, memorised all the teachings that the Buddha had ever given. People would ask him, "What did the Buddha say?" and he would reply giving a verbal account, "Thus have I heard, at one time …" This indicates that we can trust that we are encountering the actual words of the Buddha. Many western scholars suggest that Mahayana Buddhism developed 500-600 years after the death of the Buddha. But the text, by beginning in this way, asserts that this is exactly what the Buddha actually did say.

According to the tradition, there were three turnings of the wheel of the Dharma, or three perspectives on dharma taught by the Buddha. The first turning was in the Deer Park in Sarnath, near Benares. This occurred just after the Buddha's enlightenment and it was then that the Buddha taught the Four Noble Truths of suffering, the cause of suffering, the ending of suffering and the eight-fold path to the ending of suffering. Some years later he went to the Vulture Peak Hill in Rajgir, Bihar and made the second turning of the wheel. This includes the THE HEART SUTRA which sets out that all phenomena are empty of self-substance. The third turning of the wheel occurred later in the Buddha's life at Mount Malaya, in South India. On this occasion he set out the view and practices of tantra.

THE HEART SUTRA states that **the Buddha was staying at the Vulture Peak hill in Rajgir, together with a great assembly sangha of ordained monks and bodhisattvas**. In this text the 'sangha of the monks' indicates the followers of the hinayana tradition. The 'sangha of the bodhisattvas' indicates the followers of the mahayana tradition. Hinayana means lesser vehicle, small vehicle. Mahayana means a big vehicle. The polite name for hinayana is theravada, the vehicle of the elders, the path of the elders. The key point is that these two groups, the monks of the hinayana and of the bodhisattvas of the mahayana, are sitting together even though they had clear differences of approach. The monks are focussed on renunciation of the outer and inner factors which, as sentient beings, bind them to samsara. They strive to become calm and clear. The bodhisattvas are focused on seeing the emptiness of all phenomena and through that working for the liberation of all beings.

The text states that **at that time, Bhagavan was resting evenly in the absorbed contemplation known as 'Profound Illumination' which discerns the nature of phenomena**. Bhagavan in this context refers to Buddha Shakyamuni. He is in deep meditation with no disturbance. He enters the state in which everything which arises in the mind is the illumination arising from the natural clarity of the mind. Every experience is the mind's own intrinsic radiance. This is the true nature of all phenomena.

When we look around this room we see many things, and each thing is different from ourselves. Yet each of us sitting here is experiencing ourselves and the room simultaneously. We dont experience ourselves first and then the room or the room first and then ourselves. Rather we experience ourselves and the room together. What we call the room, the floor, the table, the chair, my nose, my feet – all of this arises as experience. Sensation is experience, memory is experience, thought is experience. This is all there is. Within the frame of duality there appears to be an experiencer, ourselves, and what is experienced, everything else. The sense of ourselves is actually fluctuating and sometimes it seems to be the experiencer and sometimes the experienced. Both are illuminated by awareness which is neither subject nor object.

Observing clearly in this way gives us a small taste of the meditation in which the Buddha sees the nature of all phenomena. It is not something esoteric. It is exactly how it is here, moment by moment. Why does the Buddha see it and we don't? Well, it is actually what we see, but we tell ourselves that we see something different. We are so used to relying on the story we tell ourselves that the story has come to be the seal or validator of the truth of experience. Telling, rather than simply seeing, has become our way of existence. We have come to require narrative to illuminate perception even though perception exists prior to narrative. This is what we need to explore, our own reliance on narrative. We have come to believe that we, the subject, see a world of really existing objects outside ourselves. This is our habitual interpretation, and from the Buddha's point of view, it is false.

While the Buddha was abiding evenly in this deep meditation, the Great Bodhisattva Arya Avalokiteshvara was clearly observing from within the profound practice of transcendental wise discernment. The title 'Bodhisattva' indicates that he is concerned with the enlightenment of all beings and not just himself. His meditation discerns the actual nature of all phenomena, seeing directly how each is when not interpreted.

Then the text says, **through this he truly saw the natural emptiness of the five factors of composition**. These five factors are the five skandhas or pseudo-substances: form, feeling, compositional perception, aggregation and consciousness. According to the hinayana they are the basic constituents whose interaction generates our sense of actual people. They are taken to be the irreducible basic elements out of which each person arises.

Form is the first skandha and indicates shape and colour. There is an appearance which is taken to indicate the presence of a 'thing'. This is the form of something and, whether it is a tree or a cat, this is the form of something, something which has this form. The form seems to show definitively that this 'something' has an objective stability. When the presence of a form is noticed it generates a feeling which can be positive, negative or neutral and from this comes a reaction of liking, not liking or indifference. On the basis of this second skandha of sensation and feeling, the subject starts to take up a position towards the object. Following on feeling there is the third skandha, compositional perception, whereby the subjective activity composes a picture, an image, of what it is encountering. Thus I am seeing or hearing or tasting 'something' significant for me. I see *this*, touch *this*, know *this* –'this' is something I can apprehend. On the basis of *this* there is the fourth skandha, the activity of aggregation, of bringing different factors together to fill out this developing image. Memories, intentions, cultural attitudes – whatever can be associated with this image is aggregated with it to form a substantial composite. Each individual forms such aggregates according to their own history and volition and so the 'object' is now redolent with subjective value and significance. The fifth skandha is consciousness, the knowledge of constructs. Aggregates are comprehended, taken hold of by the cognitive urge to know something. This completes the process of reification of the object and the simultaneous establishment of the subject as the one who has definite knowledge of the things of this world. Someone knows something about something. This sense of someone becomes a habitual factor, arising as a seemingly stable reference point.

Yet Avalokiteshvara saw the intrinsic emptiness of the skandhas. He saw that they have no self-substance or essence. In fact our usual deluded idea of their defining essences is generated out of our concept-mediated way of experiencing them. For example, say I am kicking a ball. This is a description of an activity. "James, what are you doing?" "I am playing football." That is rather different. 'Playing football' becomes a kind of skin which we wrap around the activity. We move from a simple description of a sequence of actions, "I am kicking a ball" to "I am playing football". Football carries many symbolic connotations. By wrapping yourself in the term 'football', different kinds of meaning are evoked. The activity is the same, but the signification of football merges a transient moment into an enduring concept which makes it easier to think and talk about.

—*Mum, for Christmas I need to get a football strip because I want to play football.*

—But what are you doing now?

—*I am playing football.*

—Oh, I thought you were just kicking a ball.

—*No, mum, it is football!*

This example indicates how the concept creates the sense of an essence, of there being a real world of football which you can enter and be part of. The term 'emptiness' points to the falsity of this imagined reality. To take appearances to be the appearance of 'some-thing' is a delusion. Appearances arise due to causes and conditions and have no sustaining or defining separate 'self' essence. Everything in the world is empty of self-substance. This doesn't mean that there is nothing there at all since clearly we still see buses and planes and cats and trees. All these forms are arising as the interplay of patterns of energy. They dont each arise from an individual essence, yet the patterning of the energetic display creates shapes onto which we project the illusion of a real essence. To see that there is no individual essence to anything doesnt dissolve the world. Rather it lightens us so that our relationship with the world moves from thinking there are separate things that we can grasp, to having a sense that we are participating in an ever-unfolding display of co-emergence. Patterns without essence effortlessly give rise to new patterns. Experience arises as interaction free of definitive essence in either cause or product.

Now we are moving towards having a break. Perhaps you might want to have a cup of tea: the kettle boils, there is hot water. Cold water, due to the power of electricity, becomes hot water. Hot water poured on to a teabag releases colour and taste. You raise the cup to your lips, there is a hot liquid which has colour and taste. "Oh, a cup of tea! Just what I needed." What you get, actually, is colour and taste. What you imagine is, 'here is a cup of tea'. In this way, moment-by-moment, you can observe for yourself how you massage essentialising concepts into each situation. Then you believe it and value it and fall in love with it. The story of Pygmalion relates how an artist creates an image of a beautiful woman and then falls in love with the image as if it were a real person. What was created is taken to be self-existing. The activity of our own mind creates an illusion into which we fall and then are trapped by our having disowned our own creativity. Yet nothing has come into real existence. It is simply the play of our imagination. Samsara is created by our imagination. This does not mean that we are consciously deceiving ourselves. Rather it is that we have such a narrow ego-focused sense of our mind we cannot see that our mind is actually vast like the sky.

Taking the transitory contents of our mind to be our limit we ignore the open ground of our presence and its fecundity. Ceaselessly, effortlessly, the open empty ground displays all the experiences that we encounter – whether we take these to be outside of 'us' or inside. Our imagination is both the limited range of our ego fantasies and the whole infinity of all that occurs since we, this presence, are both finite and infinite. It is not a matter of either/or. When we relax and release our reificatory control we are present with a flow of images. This flow has no beginning or end. It is complex, interactive, co-emergent and is beyond reification, objectification and appropriation. However, when we take on our ego-identity we become part of the flow of experience. We then rely on concepts which indicate a multitude of separate real entities. The term 'house' is a concept. Under its power we think we can speak about houses as if they were real existents rather than transient composites. In this way we ourselves fragment the world and diminish our sense of who and how we are. Ignoring the truth of our unborn openness we live a lie and so must face the sufferings of old age, sickness and death.

THE HEART SUTRA text describes how the Buddha is meditating and Avalokiteshvara is also meditating: **through the power of the Buddha, the venerable Shariputra spoke as follows to the Bodhisattva-Mahasattva Arya Avalokiteshvara**. The depth and clarity of the Buddha's mind encompasses all dharma and finds no real conflict between hinayana and mahayana views and practices. His skilful means bring about dialogue and collaboration where there might appear to be irreconcilable difference.

Thus Shariputra asks, **"In what manner should they train, those of good family who wish to follow the profound practice of transcendental wise discerning?"** In a sense he is asking, "How should we approach understanding the world as it truly is? In our level of practice, we are used to analysing people in terms of the five skandhas so that we don't feel attachment to them. But we have heard that you follow a method different from our kind of analysis." The problem with analysis is that it comes after the fact, after the event has occurred. This keeps us shuffling between past, present and future without being present in the here and now. Shariputra is asking, "Can you show me how to go beyond this?"

The Bodhisattva-Mahasattva Arya Avalokiteshvara made this reply to the venerable Shariputra. We can notice here that the mahayana teacher Avalokiteshvara is given more titles than Shariputra. 'Bodhisattva' means a being who is committed to achieving enlightenment for all beings. "Mahasattva" means a great being, one who has a profound understanding of how the world actually is in its emptiness. He is an 'Arya', which means that he is pure, an elevated one from a good family, and he is proper in every way. He says to the Venerable Shariputra, **"Shariputra, whichever of those sons or daughters of a good family wish to follow the profound practice of transcendental wise discerning should look thoroughly in the manner I will describe and thus clearly see that the five skandha factors of composition are intrinsically empty of inherent self-existence."**

The term translated here as 'discerning' is often referred to as wisdom. If we say wisdom or discernment it implies a state that you arrive at or a quality which you can possess. However, discerning is actually a practice. It is a practice you can become very good at so that it becomes part of your way of being yet it is still an on-going activity. It is the activity of seeing the precise details of what is emerging and, vitally, seeing that they are all empty of inherent existence.

For example, when you are a child and are learning to ride a bicycle it is often quite difficult to find a sense of balance. Children tend to wobble a bit at first and then fall off. The gestures they make are quite rough because they are very conscious of trying to ride. They know that they should keep the bicycle straight. Perhaps the adult who is walking with them and holding the seat to stabilise them says, "Just don't rock too much, stay stable, come on, you are doing okay, keep pedalling." You are getting advice and trying to bring these nice words into your body. But of course when you are trying to think about advice, it takes you out of your body. It is difficult to hear advice and take it straight into the body.

Discerning is like finding your balance when riding a bicycle. Once you can ride a bicycle on the road, you can start to go off the road into the field and manage the bumps on the earth as you take the whole of your body into the process of balancing. Balance is established and dissolved moment by moment. Similarly, wise discerning is a continuous activity of following the Middle Way between all extremes. By not falling to left or to right, to permanence or to impermanence, to reality or to fantasy, we abide with dynamic balance, a felt sense of presence revealing the empty nature of all phenomena. Discerning is then our way of participating. We don't have to stand apart and observe and analyse. Nor are we merely caught up in the flow of experience. Discerning reveals appearance and clarity as inseparable, immediate and intrinsically empty.

Meditation is the practice of tenderness. Although our aim, our intention, our desire is to stay with the open sense of the emptiness of all phenomena, due to the arising of the power of habit and tendency, we temporarily go under the power of what is occurring. Due to this we are pulled either into blind fusion with the occurrence or into a disengaging avoidance and so lose the middle way and become lost in the jungle of desire and aversion. However true discerning lets us see that we are not fundamentally lost, for even this lostness is empty of inherent existence and so returning to aware presence is but a short distance.

The body is designed for moving; speech and breath are moving and our mind as we know it is always moving. Our existence is nothing but movement. The body is an incredible system of biochemical and electrical communication. The endocrine system, the central nervous system, the sympathetic and parasympathetic nervous systems and so on – there are so many communicative systems in the body. Each of our cells is active and connective. Without the movement of the breath our life situation becomes imperilled. And, as we know, when we sit in meditation, thoughts, feelings and sensations are always arising. Therefore it is helpful to see that movement is not the enemy. Don't try to block the movement of the mind, don't encourage it or try to direct it. Simply be open with it and it will show you its own emptiness.

If we take the bodhisattva vow, manifesting our intention to serve and help all sentient beings then there is no form of living existence which is our enemy. Our task is to find a way to relate to whatever kind of living beings we encounter. Extending the range of our movement gives us more capacity to meet the diversity of beings. Our potential is infinite. We have, however, habit formations which are finite and restrictive. When we relate to others from the patterns of our own habit formations — because we take these patterns to be what we are — we tend to try to invite others to join us in the confirmation of the validity of our patterns, and no doubt they are trying to do the same to us. With wise discerning we align with the ongoing clarity of positioning ourselves in our fresh potential rather than in our habit formation.

We can experience every aspect of life as our practice. Our life is what arrives for us and so our practice is to be with what is. Whether it is sadness, loneliness, confusion, a sense of betrayal, abandonment, jealousy, pride, whatever it is — this is our experience in this moment. It doesn't define who we are, but it is how we are as manifestation, as participation, and so this is what we have to work with.

Then, from the clarity of his meditation, Avalokiteshvara starts to explain the actuality of every situation, "**Form is empty. Emptiness is form. Emptiness is not other than from. Form is not other than emptiness.**"

I am holding a glass of water and a pen. The glass of water is not a pen because these objects are clearly different. Objects are defined through mutual exclusion: this 'thing' and that 'thing' cant be the same. The pen-ness of the pen and the glass-ness of the glass are mutually exclusive. Part of this being a pen is the very simple fact that it is not a glass of water. This is a glass of water because it is not a table, not a floor, not a carpet, not a pen. This is the law of mutual exclusion. Yet Avalokiteshvara is pointing to something different. Here is emptiness and here, simultaneously and inseparably, is form. They are not two things.

It is not that something comes out of nothing and then stands apart from it. When a baby is born it comes out of the mother's body and is now separate and different from the mother. The small person is still very dependent on the mother, but from the separation arising from cutting the umbilical cord, the small person is moving ever further into independence. Child and mother are not the same and we take them to be two different entities; they are mutually excluding when taken to be reified entities.

Emptiness and form are not two things. Emptiness is not a thing, not a substance, not an entity. It is simply the all-pervading fact of the absence of intrinsic essence, of self-substance in all phenomena. All that appears is empty like a rainbow. Form is emptiness, emptiness is form. There are not two things, nor is there just one thing. They are non-dual: neither the same nor different. When there is form there is emptiness. They are inseparable yet not merged as one. The richness and complexity of forms is as it is, and is always empty.

There is no need to put everything in a blender and homogenise it. The difference is there – a difference of appearance. Yet appearance is intrinsically empty. The differences between appearances are not underpinned by differences of inherently defining substance. All forms arise due to the interplay of multiple causes and conditions; they are not self-caused or underpinned by an internal essence. The walls of our prison— that is, our attachment, judgement, ceaseless effort and so on — are paper-thin, mere projections of our mind.

The strength and weakness of objects are relative situational qualities; they are established relationally according to the qualities of what is encountered. They are not absolute. In the old days soldiers wore metal armour which could protect them from a knife or a big sword. Nowadays there are many weapons which can go through almost any kind of armoury. The safety of soldiers is dependent on their armour relative to the weapons the other side has. All phenomena exist or manifest within relative truth: their value, function, and continuance all depend on factors extrinsic to them. The seeming hardness of a stone is relative – if I hit it with a hammer it will break but if I hit it with a plate the plate will break. The children's game of 'stone, paper, scissors' is accurate in showing the relativity of function and value.

Avalokiteshvara continues, **"In the same way feelings, perceptions, formations and consciousness are all empty."** The five skandhas or basic components of my 'existence' are all empty. Of course this doesn't mean that they don't manifest at all. It means that they don't exist in and of themselves. They are relational and relative to the factors operating around them. My mother had a mother. My mother was the daughter of her mother. How could one woman be a daughter and a mother at the same time? To me as a child this seemed ridiculous because really, this woman was my mother. Every time I saw her, I would say 'Mum, …', and she said, 'Yes, James?' She didn't say, 'I'm a daughter not a mother.' So, for me she is my mother, simply that. My father didn't have her as his mother. For my father this woman was his wife. This is very interesting. When we are children our mother is just our mother; all the other aspects of her life are irrelevant to us. Yet my mother was my mother for me, not for my father and not for her mother. The truth of her being my mother is relative; it is dependent on the fact of me being her son and not her husband and not her mother. If you have children, these are your children and you love them. To other people they are just children, who might be pleasant or unpleasant. Meaning and value are ascribed through context and function. None of the five basic components is self-existing or absolute – they are what they are due to factors beyond them – they are part of the interdependent flow of appearance.

All forms, sensations, feelings, thoughts, rocks and so on are impermanent. They arise and pass away. The five skandha constituents manifest and dissolve. Each of them is empty. Empty form arises and passes. Empty feeling, empty perception, empty association, empty consciousness. They are mere patterns of appearance without internal essence or definition. The world is like a dream and so are we.

What is the flavour of emptiness? The flavour is ungraspability. You can't find emptiness, somewhere, as something. It is the very opposite of something and it is everywhere. Although it is not a thing you can get, you can get it in a similar way to how you can get a joke. If you get a joke, you don't *get* anything - but you get the joke. You can't put it in your pocket. You get it, "Oh!" It is like that. There is nothing to get, but when you get it, you get it. So, what stops us getting it? Is it that we are already getting something else? If you're getting something that seems real it is very difficult to get nothing, which is inseparable from all somethings and which establishes them as un-real, as illusion.

Emptiness, the groundless ground of everything, exposes the seductive falsity of our sense of time as a composite of past present and future. Although we may know that we have many possessions, they are only alive for us when we are with them.

For example, I have many books but the books need me in order to show their qualities and this showing is the unfolding of time as the series of now. I pick up a book and start to read it. I turn the page; I start at the first line and work my way down to the bottom of the page and turn another page. What are we getting as we read a book? The unfolding of experience. It seems like a flow and we can think about what's happened in earlier chapters and yet the disclosure of the book is always in the ungraspable present. The now of the actuality is just this, just what is here now. The sentences flow through now, which is where we are, where we always are. In this way we can say that we have never had anything and we will never have anything, for this, so vivid, so immediate, is always already vanishing.

Lunchtime is approaching and we say, "Well, we hope we are going to get some food." Then as we eat, the food reveals itself in the moment of its destruction. It flourishes in its demise. If you watch a movie, the movie reveals itself in its vanishing. You listen to music or play music or sing or dance – these are moments of experience revealed even as they vanish.

Emptiness indicates that our lives are ungraspable. There is no essence or entity anywhere and yet we move in the sky of immediate experience and swim in the ocean of immediate experience. What I call 'I, me, my, myself' is itself experience. The experiencer and the experience are both experienced. So, who is the real experiencer? This is the true focus of dzogchen.

The focus of our meditation is the non-duality of stillness and movement. The 'contents' of the mind are always moving; new experiences are always arising. What is stillness? In some approaches to meditation it is considered to be the fruit of practice. They say that you have to still your mind. However, the mind itself never moves. To use a traditional image, the mind is like a mirror. The mirror doesn't change in any way in itself, yet it shows many different reflections.

Similarly when we are sitting here many experiences arise. Memories, plans for the future, sensations in the body – different experiences arise and pass. Yet open empty awareness does not change. If you relax into the presence of awareness you will be still and untainted by anything that occurs. Profound stillness is simple and inherent whereas change is contingent and unpredictable.

When we cut the thread of narrative and interpretation, each event is itself here for a moment and then gone. This is not chaotic. If you have a necklace and cut the thread, all the beads will scatter. But when we cut the thread of narrative each moment is just where it is, self-arising and self-passing. Calm and clear. The integrity of experience is maintained not by organising it, not by editing or making intentional choices to compose specific sequences. In fact, appearance is self-organising due to the intrinsic clarity of the mind.

When we are not in touch with this clarity aspect of being present as awareness, we find ourselves identifying with ego-consciousness and then tend to mobilise our intelligence, our knowledge, our energy to make sense of 'things'. We feel a need to make meaning by interpreting our impressions of what is occurring. This involves selective attention with a tendency to privilege what is familiar to us. The freshness of the situation offers many possibilities, but if I am relying on concepts I don't have time to run through all the options. Instead I impulsively go for a familiar explanatory idea that seems to give me access to the aspects of the field that I need in order to carry forward my intention. Being a busy person I don't want to be surprised at the wonder of the world – I just want to do what I feel I have to do. When the complexity of the facts puts my map into question it often seems easier to ignore the facts and hang on to the map.

For example, let's imagine we are in an art class and we are going to draw this chair. Can everybody see this chair? Do we agree, this is a chair? Any other ideas? Okay? So for us, this is a chair. Each of us tries to draw what we see. Yet because we are seated in different parts of the room, we each get a different view of the chair. So the drawings we make are rather different. We agree that we are drawing 'the same chair' yet what we see in the drawings are seemingly different chairs. Which view of the chair is the right one? Which one reveals the chair as it actually is? Drawings give an impression of the chair as we see it and these impressions are then evaluated in terms of our concepts, including our concept of 'what the chair looks like'. The chair itself is manifest, tangible, revelatory – but not definable or graspable. However we try to represent it, our representation is always something new, something other than the immediacy aspect of the chair as we see it.

This is the root freedom of existence. Art illuminates this again and again. The world is beyond appropriation. Each drawing, painting, sculpture is a gesture within the flow of gestures of appearance. There can be no conclusion to the process of representation since no gesture is final. Concepts create the illusion of graspable objects that can be fully and finally grasped but the fullness of the unfolding field of experience has a richness and diversity that evades all organising concepts. Phenomena are just as they are, yet they are in excess, in terms of the lack inherent in concepts.

The seeming sameness of objects across time is dependent upon our capacity to apply the same concept to situations which are merely similar. Our capacity to apply concepts is the continuity of our world. The Tibetan word for consciousness is nampar shepa. 'Nampar' means a distinct part, an apprehendable entity, and 'shepa' means to know. This indicates that we know the knowability of things. We know appearances not in the immediacy of their visual form but in terms of their conceptualised form, the form that is given to them by the concepts we use to describe 'them'. The concept used to name and apprehend the appearance gives birth to their entity-for-us. Before the concept is applied there is no entity.

The object of consciousness is concepts. We think that we think about the chair. But we don't. We think about our idea of the chair, for we cannot think about the chair itself as it is veiled by our projections. The chair we think about is the chair we imagine. If you are an artist, you can draw the chair a thousand times yet you will never arrive at the 'real' chair. The concept of chair allows the simplification of the complexity of the actual. This simplification is the means by which we delude ourselves and so happily abide in our fantasy of mastery over the world. Our ego seeks this simplification but our awareness does not need it. In fact, conceptual simplification veils our clarity so that in the resulting dullness we cling to concepts rather than opening to unborn awareness.

Life is always fresh if you simply see, and it is always stale if you rely on thoughts. Thought patterns may seem fresh but they keep us within the paradigm of interpretation, and interpretation involves applying thoughts that we are already familiar with, layering the past over the present. Comparing and contrasting covers over the bright freshness of the unrepeatable moment.

When THE HEART SUTRA says that the five constituent skandhas are empty, it points to their potential, to their indeterminacy. Instead of using them to consolidate our position we can play with their illusory formation, enjoying immediacy, spontaneity and freshness. Be with however experience is occurring for you. Be with experience as it is. Don't overcook it. Be with your sadness, your happiness, your intimacy, your loneliness: whatever is arising, this is how this moment is. We don't know how long we will live or how long situations will last. We can make plans, have hopes and so on, but none of us knows what will come. However, if we give ourselves fully to what is here, we will find that each moment is complete. It is what it is and we are fully here.

Therefore it is vital not to cut off into the realm of editing, judging, managing and selecting. We are giving ourselves in openness and the world is giving itself fully as it is. This meeting of open to open, of sky to sky, is the non-duality, the intrinsic completeness of the moment. However if we get frightened and retreat away from how it is, we don't find ourselves in a safe haven. Not trusting our capacity to participate in openness and collaborate with circumstances, we find ourselves in the nowhere land of control where we are endlessly manipulating interpretations so that our activity fulfils our egoic intentions. Relying on conceptualisation we see the options of different pathways and different possible scenarios and, remembering the old saying, 'Don't put all your eggs in one basket', we hedge our bets. We have a diverse portfolio existence in which we sustain a bit of this and a bit of that.

However if you never fully open to this precious transient moment then life is diminished in its richness and vitality. Fear is a poor guide to life. Devotion is the basis of tantra, an open-hearted devotion in which we give ourselves to the meditation deity 100%. If this is our path then we must trust that it is enough and therefore there is no need to hedge our bets or hold something back 'just in case'. We give everything we have and everything we are to the practice because what is at stake is the danger of staying trapped inside our own thoughts, staying trapped inside our fear. We give all to gain all. This is not sacrifice but letting go of concepts in order to find our own ever-present true nature.

Emptiness means seeing the impermanent shimmering immediate nature of thought, seeing that there is nothing to grasp. Moreover, the grasper has no substance. The grasper is an illusion arising from the linking of hundreds of moments of merging with grasping thoughts. Who does that immersion and identification? No one. There is no real ego self, no real separate autonomous doer or maker. Ideas are forms of energy which can be further imbued with energy. This thickens them until they operate as entities. Subject and object are ideas. No-one is doing this.

Energy moving in the dark manifests as sentient beings. Energy moving in the light manifests as buddhas. There are no really existing people or sentient beings or entities anywhere. There never have been and there never will be. If you bracket off all your familiar narratives of how you exist and lead your life and try to do what you want to do and what you feel you have to do, then you can observe the process of emergence. The version of this closest to our familiar conventions is the view of dependent co-origination: on the basis of 'this', 'that' arises.

In tantra we see everything as the illusory appearance of the mandala and all of occurrence as the display of the buddha. In dzogchen the open empty luminous base effortlessly gives rise to the magical illusory transient appearances that are themselves the clarity of the mind. There is no one to blame, no one to be held accountable, no persecutors and no victims, simply unborn energy displaying ceaseless patterns.

Rather than judgement and partiality, in directly seeing the open empty equalness of all occurrences, the mind settles in equanimity. With this we relax and allow each occurrence to arise and pass, arise and pass without involvement. As subject and object lose their entity-ness and are clearly mere patterns of energy, the glue of love and hate that kept them interacting in the game of winning and losing thins and dissolves and true selfless non-dual spontaneity is unimpeded. All arisings and all experiences go free by themselves as we relax and open to our intrinsic clarity which is like the mirror. The mirror just shows; the mirror doesn't organise or edit or manage, it just shows.

Now we see with a different kind of intelligence, not the intelligence based on building up systems, but the intelligence of freshness. This is the simplicity of the clarity of awareness – a simple showing with no need for egoic involvement or avoidance or control.

Unlike conceptual clarity which comes from constructing new interpretations, this clarity releases the ossification which occurs when you hold on to concepts as if they were your saviour. Form is emptiness, emptiness is not other than form. Because each form, each moment, is empty, there is no entity there to provide a basis for judgement. If we like something we say it is good, but that does not establish any permanent truth. It is merely our opinion at this particular time and in this particular place. The event is empty, as is the opinion. 'Being empty' means that each form offers no actual hooks or supports for projections or interpretations. What seems to arise as object and what seems to arise as our subjective response are both empty illusions. They are only 'real' within our delusion. Each form appears, yet cannot be subsumed in a noun and so there is no fixed thing for adjectives and adverbs to hover around. Appearance is as it appears – this is clarity. What appears cannot be turned into something else. If we act on it with our opinions and concepts and seem to develop something new, this is merely a new delusion devoid of essence. It does not touch or actually obscure the simple pure appearance that has already vanished. Samsara is the realm of ideas, of imagined entities. It does not exist except in as much as it is believed in.

THE HEART SUTRA points to this when it says that there is no development, no path, no progress, no enlightenment. There is nothing to be gained. There is nothing existing somewhere else that we need to get to in order to be okay forever. That is delusion. Looking at empty phenomena and truly awakening to their emptiness, their bright clarity is your bright clarity. The self-liberation of phenomena is the self-liberation of both subject and object – and this reveals that they themselves were modes of clarity all along. All that arises, whether as seeming objects in the world or as seeming thoughts and feelings in the mind, is devoid of inherent self-existence. All appearances arise as emptiness, and pass as emptiness. There is no gain. There is no loss.

Seeing this, living this, is the dharmakaya, the radiant presence of the Buddha's mind. It is enough. With it there is satisfaction, contentment, peace. Nothing has to change. The answer doesn't lie in the object. Letting go of that hope and projection allows space for our mind to reveal itself, arising like the sun at the dawn of day, illuminating all and dissolving the shadows of delusion.

Avalokiteshvara continues, saying to Shariputra, **"Thus, Shariputra, in that way all phenomena are themselves emptiness. They are free of signs and identification."** Whatever appears, whether to any of your senses or as your mental activity, is devoid of any substance or essence defining what it is. The status of what appears depends on whether you see clearly or whether you interpret on the basis of your familiar concepts, signs and symbols.

When your experience of the world is mediated through signs, these signs blind you to the actuality of what is there. Appearances, all phenomena as they actually are, are free of signs and the impact of language. What we think and say about 'things' does not establish any truth in these things. Thingness is an opacity, a screen veiling the bright actuality of appearance. Phenomena are not things. We impute thingness to phenomena and then we deceive ourselves by believing in their real existence. Phenomena are empty of inherent self-existence and this emptiness is free of signs. 'Free of signs' does not mean that there are no signs. It means the signs are there, they arise and pass, yet they don't touch or contaminate emptiness. Another way of saying this is to say that all signs point towards emptiness.

For example, when you look in a mirror you see reflections. But we can also say that the mirror is free of reflections. If I hold a mirror in my hand and turn it, then many different reflections arise and pass. These reflections are in the mirror but they are not identical with the mirror. When you move the mirror, the reflection that was there is instantly gone. It doesn't hide inside the mirror like a mouse going back into its hole. The mirror itself is not changed by the reflection. If you have a piece of paper and draw on it with charcoal it is very difficult to remove the marks because they are merged into the surface of the paper. However, the mirror shows reflections and is simultaneously free of reflections since it is untouched by these reflections.

This metaphor helps us to see the relation between appearances which are empty of self, and signs which seem to establish some essence or self or reality in appearances. For example, when we use the term 'table' and believe that it refers to a real table, the potential of the pieces of wood to become many different forms are hidden by the power of the sign 'table'. Once the term 'table' captures the object it is taken to be simply a table and nothing else. However if we see that emptiness is free of signs, we can still apply signs, but lightly, as gestures of communication with those who are committed to the real existence of the table-ness of the table. We can remain clear that the actual appearances can support many different signs and interpretations. The 'table' is also 'firewood' and also a 'sailing ship', 'a castle'... on and on, new visions of its potential arise.

Our conventional use of language binds signs to appearances and allocates them a seemingly given identity. When we rely on this social convention we can feel competent in the world and at ease in the flow of names and definitions. Yet none of these appearances has any true essence of its own and the imputation of such an essence conveyed by the sign merely marks culture and its assumptions as a mode of delusion, for it does not establish real entities. The presenting phenomena are ungraspable. When I employ the sign, I grasp the sign, I don't grasp the actual phenomenon that the sign claims to stand for, since all phenomena are empty.

Avalokiteshvara says, "**They are unborn and unceasing, without stain and without freedom from stains, and are without decrease or completion.**" I have a shirt and I have a cup of coffee. If I pour the coffee over my shirt it will make a dark stain. The shirt has one colour and the coffee will add another. Now the shirt is dirty, it is spoiled. The shirt had a relative purity, a purity that could be spoiled by putting something else onto it. But emptiness is without stains because there is no substance to it. Stains and marks arise when two entities meet and one leaves an impression on the other, i.e. A marks B. But emptiness itself is not an A in relation to a B – it cannot be stained. Moreover, it is without freedom from stain; its purity is not one which is maintained by holding itself apart. Everything occurs as it does, arising, showing itself and departing. These occurrences or appearances are here, present. Yet they cause no harm and leave no trace. Emptiness requires no freedom from stains since nothing can stain it. This is primordial purity. When a reflection arises in a mirror, it does not harm the mirror. The reflection is in the mirror but it is not making a mark or leaving a trace. The reflection is in the mirror, yet is not taking up residence in the mirror.

If you have a ball of crystal and put it on a red cloth, the ball looks as if it is red. If you put it on blue cloth, it will appear to be slightly blue. The crystal ball has not become red or blue, but it appears to be so, according to these circumstances. In the same way anger or sadness or any feeling can arise in our mind. Then my sense is 'I am angry', 'I am sad'. I seem to be suffused with and pervaded by this intense feeling. It is who I am. And then it is gone. I was 'stained' by it, I took on that colouration – and then it was gone and the space of awareness took on a new colouration. The mark or stain was there yet awareness is unstained. The 'stain' was itself empty of inherent existence and so intrinsically incapable of leaving a stain.

The one who appears to be stained is our ego, our capacity to fuse and identify with whatever is occurring. The ego applies the sign 'anger' to the transient feeling. The feeling passes but the ego is able to hang on to the sign and use it to develop both immediate arousal and an enduring narrative: 'What you said to me yesterday made me really angry'. This construction is itself empty of real existence yet the beguiling power of the sign creates the delusional sense that something really bad happened: 'You did something bad to me.' The sign never touches emptiness or actual phenomena. But it does touch and mark and interweave with other signs, the signs constitutive of our ego self. Although these signs are taken by dualistic consciousness to indicate a 'real' event which 'stains' the form of my existence, these created stains are empty and so there are no real stains and no freedom from such stains.

If you think, "Oh, I don't want to be like this, I shouldn't be like this. If I am getting angry that means that there is something about me which is not right. I have to do something about it", your own empty open mind is staining itself with illusory stains. There is no actual stain, yet when we believe that there is one, this generates the need to make effort to remove the stain. From the very beginning, everything which is occurring is the radiance of the mind. The seeming existence of the ego is generated solely by denying that it is part of the radiance. The fact that this illusory ego likes some things and doesn't like others generates a deluding interpretation of true value belonging to the 'object'. It is the tail wagging the dog. The ego's interpretation is actually the radiance of the mind. What the ego takes to be a stain is the radiance of awareness. What the ego takes to be perfect is the radiance of awareness. All the judgements, decisions, definitions made by the ego are powerless to bring even one really existing thing into existence. All that arises is illusion – to say that one illusion is better than another is like saying one shadow is better than another.

The text then goes through traditional lists of the items that seem to constitute our existence and points out that each of these items is empty of anything which might be its inherent existence or self. The details of these traditional lists are only meaningful if you actually use them on a daily basis to make sense of your life and your world. If you normally believe in them and take them to be true then seeing their emptiness is liberating. But if this is not the case for you then you have an additional task. Take some paper and write down the objects, concepts, feelings, memories and so on that you rely on to give you your sense of who you are and of how your world is. When you find these building blocks that generate your sense of familiar territory, observe how each is actually present for you only for a moment. My parents are empty. My children are empty. My possessions are empty. My body is empty. My youth is empty. My beauty is empty. My age is empty. My sickness is empty. These items, these people, and these qualities are present when we are in actual contact with them. They shine by the activation of our attention – otherwise they are like balloons in a pack – they need the breath of our belief to manifest their potential.

Experience itself is fleeting, yet the concepts by which we seem to apprehend experience appear to be enduring and to refer to items that continue to exist despite their vanishing. Now you are at the crossroads – do you turn towards the path of direct yet ephemeral, ungraspable experience or do you turn towards the path of reifying concepts and the delusion that they engender? Experience in the here and now is all we actually have; the past has gone, the future has not yet come, and this moment is ungraspable. By opening fully to this, the infinity of the mind inseparable from emptiness is effortlessly revealed. The mind is empty, its contents are empty, everything is empty appearance, and here we are, relaxed, open and alive. We are infinite and beyond definition. This is our primordial freedom. However we are is merely the current patterning of the effervescent energy of our open mind.

Avalokiteshvara continues to Shariputra, "**Emptiness is without form, without feeling, without perception, without formation and without consciousness; without eye, without ear, without nose, without tongue, without body, without mentation; without form, without sound, without smell, without taste, without sensation, and without objects of mentation. Emptiness is without the domain of vision and without the domain of the other senses up to and including the domain of mentation.**" This is a traditional categorization: the six senses, including the mind as an organising faculty, the six sense organs, including the heart, the organ of the mind, and the six consciousnesses. Emptiness is without all of these constituent factors. They are illusion. They appear and function as illusion. They are empty of inherent existence and so emptiness is free of them since they are neither just the same as emptiness nor truly different from it.

For example, a mirror is without reflections in the sense that it has no single essential defining reflection. The mirror doesn't show itself in the reflection, yet its clarity shows as reflection. What it shows is within it yet is not it – and is also not not it. In the same way, emptiness shows form, shape, colour, it shows our eyes, our ears, our tongue.

All of this is arising, yet when we look without relying on concepts we see that these are mere empty experiences, like a mirage or a rainbow. Sensation arises and vanishes and yet, being without self-substance, it neither arises nor vanishes. Everything that we call internal, everything that we call external and everything at our senses, the meeting point of the external and the internal, is empty. This is expressed in the tradition in terms of what are called 'The Three Wheels'. The object is empty, the subject is empty and the relation between them is empty. We are ceaselessly manifesting as ungraspable movements. **"And emptiness is without all the domains of consciousness up to and including mentation consciousness."**

Avalokiteshvara says, "**Emptiness is free of ignorance, and of the extinction of ignorance and of all twelve factors of dependent co-arising up until old age and death and the extinction of old age and**

death." These are the twelve stages of dependent origination which are depicted in the Tibetan Wheel of Life (see page 85).

The twelve conditioning links or nidanas are: ignorance, formation, consciousness, name-and-form, six sense organs, contact, feeling, craving, clinging, becoming, birth, old age and death. Although as a wheel, a circle, it has no beginning or end, conventionally the cycle is taken to commence with ignorance which is depicted as a blind, old woman. Ignorance is represented as a woman, because woman, the feminine, represents wisdom. She is old, because wisdom is primordial, but she's also blind. When the dulling power of ignoring how life actually is manifests as a deluded sense of the duality of subject and object then this preoccupation blinds us to the light of awareness. Ignorance is the not seeing or the ignoring of what is here, as it is corrupted with the simultaneous belief in false ideas about how it is. On the basis of this ignoring, there is confusion and the consequent struggle to make sense of what is happening.

The next image is of a potter's wheel representing formation. In India, potters work with a big wooden wheel that is very heavy. In the middle they have a mountain of clay and they use a stick to turn the wheel. The wheel goes round and builds up a lot of momentum, and then the potter works on the clay at the top of this pile. From this mass of clay they make a little pot, like a little teacup. It appears poised at the top and then it is cut free. So, there is the mass and this new shape. The shape is formed of the mass; they are of one flesh, part unformed, part formed. Then they are cut apart and now there is a cup. This image stands for mental formation, whereby we construct the forms of the world. The mass of clay is all our potential, our habits, assumptions, memories, knowledge – a latent richness inseparable from the ground of emptiness. With this an idea arises and takes form – and suddenly the cup appears as something existing in and of itself.

Once the shape of the cup is cut free from the mass of clay, its origin is forgotten and it is just itself, timelessly itself. In this way, ignoring the ever-present ground leads us to the sense that we are a thing among things. I am me, just me, simply me. I feel myself to be entire, to be singular and individual – despite all the evidence to the contrary. My moods shift, my sensations change, the events around me alter my possibilities and actions. I breathe in the air of the world and depend on food and drink – yet I still feel, 'Well I'm just me whatever happens.' This sense of an unchanging basic identity, an essence, leads me to be self-protective and self-aggrandising. My belief in my self, in my core, is strange because it is impossible to describe this core. In Tibetan it is referred to as *bDag-'Dzin*, grasping at I or ego, or holding on to self. The paradox is that it is the grasping, the activity of identifying, investing, holding on to and so on which actually creates the delusion that there is an already existing I or self that one is attached to. Separating from the flow of dependent origination, from the ground of emptiness, is a mental activity which must be repeated again and again – for only by its repetition can the delusion of separation be maintained. Samsara is generated by our own busy mind. Nirvana is revealed when we let go of the self-appointed task of maintaining the activity of ignoring how it is.

The first two of the twelve linked steps establish the frame of reference within which the other ten operate. Ignoring means forgetting the immediacy of the field and retreating into reliance on concepts which are themselves always part of the flow. Then formation arises as the activity of solidifying concepts and using them to formulate descriptions of seemingly separate entities. This is the basis for all the lostness that we experience in our lives. Trusting that we are able to define both subject and object we gain confidence in our own knowledge, in our capacity and in our competence. We are creatures who live by the recognition of patterns and the capacity to predict future patterns. This creates a misleading pseudo-clarity that has us endlessly chasing after empty appearances which we think and talk about as being actual entities.

Then Avalokiteshvara says, **"Similarly, emptiness is free of suffering, its cause, its cessation and the path that leads to the cessation of suffering."** The Four Noble Truths, the foundation of buddhism, are empty! This is challenging, for it is dissolving not only misleading worldly certainties but vital dharma certainties. Suffering is empty. The cause of suffering is empty as well. Empty indicates that they are not self-existing, not true in themselves. They are relatively true, depending on circumstances. Suffering is experience, and experience is impermanent and contingent. The cause of suffering is ignorance and ignorance is not a fixed state but is actually the ceaseless activity of ignoring. Ignoring what is actual and fleeting by attending to what is not, that is to illusion. By taking illusion to be real one is immersed in delusion, which is the certainty that self-existing entities, including ourselves, are real.

But where is the substance of this? We suspend disbelief and are taken in by the theatre of samsara. Drama after drama captivates us – yet nothing has truly happened – it is like a dream or a mirage. This itself is a terrible truth – we are trapped in a prison made of clouds. It is our own fear and habitual reifying perception that creates the seeming solidity that traps us. Nothing is ever established. All phenomena are empty. They have no personal essence to them. Seeing this there is no need to remove the cause of suffering since it is already empty. The road maintenance department may have snow-ploughs but it has no machine for removing mirages! The eightfold noble path is empty. The one necessity is to stay with the one who gets lost. Stay with the one who gets confused. Look at your own mind and keep looking until you see its own empty nature.

Our faults and limitations are a quality of clarity, of the energy or illusory appearance of our empty mind. However, the fact that they are a quality of clarity doesn't mean that they are the same as generosity and compassion. Everything is empty, everything has the same nature, the same basic taste of emptiness, yet this doesn't mean that we can take samsara into the kitchen and put all its diversity into the blender to make juice that all has the same flavour! Everything that occurs has the same taste of emptiness and each appearance has the precise unique taste of its specificity in this specific moment. Kindness is kind, tolerance is tolerant, love is love, hate is hate, jealousy is jealousy. Each of these has a different taste. Everything tastes as it is. When we are cruel, this is cruelty and emptiness. This is true. But the fact that cruelty is empty doesn't stop it being cruel. So it is very important to have both wisdom – the truth of the emptiness of all phenomena – and compassion, openly relating to the specificity of each being. Our wisdom should be like the sky, infinite. Our compassion should be as fine as the point of a needle.

The five elements are empty. The five constituent skandhas are empty, the eighteen constructive parts are empty, the twelve links of the chain of dependent origination are empty, the four noble truths are empty. Everything is empty, but that does not mean that it is nothing at all. We follow the Middle Way between eternalism and extinction. To open to emptiness is to uncover the brightness of life. Form is emptiness, emptiness is not other than form. Compassion and wisdom are inseparable, like the two wings of a bird. If the bird only has one wing, it can't fly.

Then Avalokiteshvara says, **"Emptiness is free of intrinsic original knowing and is free of attainment and also of non-attainment."** There is nothing to get and nowhere better to be. Whether heaven or hell arises for you, stay relaxed and open in awareness inseparable from emptiness. There is no gain or loss. The mirror is empty. It has always been empty and always will be empty. The myriad reflections which arise in it do not affect that emptiness in any way for they also are empty. Patterns have their own distinct qualities as they manifest yet none separates out and becomes something in itself. Everything is always already empty. There is nothing to do except be with this. And we find ourselves being with this when we awaken from the delusion that we have to do something, to make our individual mark. There is nothing for us to do, nothing to strive for; no gain, no loss.

Awareness does not make anything. The ego-self is itself an illusory construct – it is not truly made nor can it make anything. Appearance arises like a dream – unborn and unceasing, free of the veil of belief in separate existence. Spontaneous manifestation is not random, for intrinsic knowing intuits the fitting gesture which manifests without egoic effort. Free of the false duality of subject and object there is just the simplicity of how it is, as it is. When we think we have arrived somewhere better, this is simply a thought operating in the matrix of compare and contrast. If you take refuge in thoughts they will take you somewhere – yet that somewhere is itself nowhere, it is empty, an illusory pattern in the semiotic web. There is no safer place to get to. Primordial emptiness is the only safe space and it is here already.

Then Avalokiteshvara says, **"Therefore Shariputra, because there is nothing to be gained, bodhisattvas rely on transcendental wise discerning, and dwelling with minds free of obscuration, are without fear. Having passed completely from the domain of deception, they attain the full release of nirvana."** There is nothing to attain. We are not on a spiritual path, we are not on a journey, we are not going anywhere. Being right here, being where we are, being present, this is the ground and the path and the result. There is no better place to be.

Perhaps you could learn to play Tibetan musical instruments, you could learn sacred dances, you could memorise pages of rituals, you could learn mudras, learn how to make tormas and so on. None of these activities will take you anywhere other than where you are right now. Where are you? We are here, now. Relaxing into the presence of our ever-available awareness is the one key point. Each moment is completely and fully itself and being present with this is intrinsic satisfaction. Wanting more or less or different is play, if non-dual, and is endless samsara, if dual. The desire for change arises from dissatisfaction, from the feeling of lack or excess. With this you can, in your identification as subject, change the furniture in your outer and inner habitation but you will still be relying on concepts to work out where you are. Your home will be a narrative.

One's whole life can be spent like this. Yet we are here in infinite space. This is the dharmadhatu, the space of phenomena as they are. This is the womb of the great mother that we have never left. So don't confuse furniture with space. Qualities are relative, as are symbols and signs. The mind itself is not relative, it is empty and infinite. Everything that occurs anywhere at any time occurs in the dharmadhatu, the infinite space inseparable from awareness, so rest in the dharmadhatu and find that everything is present without effort. There is no attainment. Seeing this we relax, forever free of delusion.

Then Avalokiteshvara says, **"All buddhas abiding in the three times also rely on transcendental wise discerning and thus, with unexcelled, perfect awakening, are completely enlightened buddhas."** There is no other method for awakening. All buddhas follow this way which is not a way to go or to come. So letting go of coming and going we are at one with the buddhas. In order to rest, to be at ease where we are, we need to be inseparable from space, from unborn emptiness. To do this we have the help of the great mantra of transcendent wise discernment. Mantras protect our mind from our own habitual tendencies to be caught up in the fleeting content of our minds.

Avalokiteshvara then says that **"This is the mantra of transcendental wise discerning, the mantra of great awareness, the unsurpassed** mantra. This is the mantra which balances the unbalanced. This is the mantra which completely pacifies all suffering. This is not deception, so you can come to know that it is true." The function of mantra is energetic not cognitive. There is no end to thinking. My teacher used to say again and again, "You can't think your way out of samsara." Mantra creates a mood in which you don't go after thoughts. You are present in your senses with an aesthetic vitality. The breath settles, the muscles relax, and you are present. The truth of the practice is an experiential truth. Without practice it is only words.

Then Avalokiteshvara says, **"Recite the mantra of transcendental wise discerning: *TADYATHA OM GATE GATE PARAGATE PARASAMGATE BODHI SVAHA.*"** In English this is, **"In this way, gone, gone, gone beyond, fully gone beyond. Awakened – as it is!"** But don't cling to the meaning of the words. Enter into the sound, find the non-duality of sound and emptiness and this will reveal the non-duality of awareness and emptiness. What have we gone beyond? We have gone beyond resting inside our limits. We enter infinity within which all limits arise and pass without causing limitation.

Then Avalokiteshvara says, **"Shariputra, in this way, a Bodhisattva-Mahasattva should train in profound transcendental wise discerning."** That is the end of Avalokiteshvara's teaching.

Then the text says, "**Then Bhagawan arose from his absorbed contemplation and praised the Bodhisattva-Mahasattva Arya Avalokitesvara, saying: *'Very good. Very good. Son of a good family, it is like that. It is like that, and so profound transcendental wise discerning is to be practised just as you have shown it. All the Tathagatas will rejoice in that.'*"** The Buddha confirms that what has been said is valid and should be practised just as described. Neither doubt nor critical commentary will lead anywhere useful. This is it. We are here, yet where are we? If we look in the manner just described we will certainly see the primordial unchanging nature, the ending of delusion. All the methods of tantra and mahamudra and dzogchen don't go beyond this. Emptiness is the heart of practice. It is enough.

The text concludes, "**Bhagawan spoke thus, and then the venerable Shariputra and the bodhisattva Avalokitesvara and all of their retinues, and all the gods, men, jealous gods, local spirits and so on of the world rejoiced and sincerely praised the speech of the**

Bhagawan Buddha." Whether you have a busy mind and live in a city running here and there, or you live in the country with a very peaceful mind, you still have stuff. Changing the quality of stuff we encounter keeps us busy – it is simply distraction. However according to this teaching, if you recognise that all stuff is empty then this emptiness is itself the immediacy of enlightenment. You don't have to simplify anything, because everything has already been simple from the very beginning. It is emptiness.

Appendix 1

Other books by James Low

1. The Open Door of Emptiness

(Published by Simply Being, UK, 2023. ISBN: 978-1739938178)

This book contains a selection of edited public talks given by James Low. Although the word 'emptiness' can seem a bit intimidating, in the Buddhist traditions it is the key to freedom. Our mind is intrinsically empty of self and any fixed or defining content. We are not defined by anything which has occurred, that is occurring now, or will even occur in the future. Being empty of fixed content allows us to open to all that occurs without being trapped in reactivity. By resting in the intrinsic openness of our mind it becomes clear that we are not a thing amongst things.

2. Buddha Shows the Way: a collection of public talks and teachings

(Published by Simply Being, UK, 2022. ISBN:979-8825841762)

This book contains a selection of edited public talks given by James Low. They cover a wide range of topics yet share a common theme: how to apply Buddhist teachings in our complex engagement with the modern world. We are all faced with ever increasing tasks of life maintenance as we struggle to cope with the profound impact of climate change, conflict, economic chaos, environmental and political instabilities. Moreover our own inner life is prey to habitual tendencies, impulses and blind spots so that our sense of the world is often more muddled than we imagine it to be.

The Buddhist view encourages us to see the ungraspable illusory nature of every situation in order that we might avoid being buffeted by samsara's waves of hopes and fears. With this clarity our own potential can be turned towards the benefit of the many rather than towards individual selfish pursuits. *The Buddha shows the way* contains eighteen short chapters which can be read in any order so it is a book that can be dipped into according to your mood and time available.

3. Proud Little Cloud: letting in the light

(Published by Simply Being, UK, 2022. ISBN: 978-0956923998)

This illustrated book invites children to see how by collaborating together, the sea and the sun and the clouds make our bright and variegated world. Each needs the other and so the key theme is that none of us is alone and we all get along better with friendly and appreciative participation.

The hope is that adults read the book aloud and talk about the pictures and these themes with the child.

4. Me First!: an account of the rise of the Wrathful Buddhas

(Published by Simply Being, UK, 2022. ISBN: 978-0956923981)

This is a traditional Tibetan epic tale of the havoc created by the arrogant entitlement that proclaims, "Me first!". When pride turns demonic, the Buddhas manifest many faces of kindness (both peaceful and wrathful) to tidy up the mess.

The text by James Low is based on the *Padma bKa'-Thang* by Padmasambhava and revealed by the terton, Urgyen gLing-Pa.

5. Sweet Simplicity: Mahamudra doha songs

(Published by Simply Being, UK, 2022. ISBN: 978-1739938154)

The beautiful brief Buddhist songs in this book point towards the inexpressible sweet simplicity of our own minds. This simplicity is usually obscured by the complexity of our reified experience and the conceptual elaboration we employ to try to work out who we are and what our life is for.

The doha songs encourage us to turn towards our own minds as the ungraspable simplicity of the ever-present ground.

The dohas here arose from the minds of enlightened yogis in Eastern India during the 8th -10th centuries. The collection is referred to as the *Asta Doha Kosa* in Sanskrit, *Do-Ha mDzod brGyad* in Tibetan. The collection is supplemented by the famous Mahamudra Aspiration prayer, also known as the Chagchen Monlam (Phyag-Chen sMon-Lam in Tibetan), written by the third Karmapa. The introduction and translation from Tibetan is by James Low.

It has been translated into German, Spanish, Italian and Hungarian.

6. Lotus Source: becoming Lotus Born

(Published by Simply Being, UK, 2021. ISBN: 978-1739938123)

This book focuses on Padmasambhava, the Lotus Born Guru, known in Tibet as Guru Rinpoche. He awakens us to our own lotus source.

All Buddhist practice is concerned with awakening from the illusions which bind us. The lotus represents both this awakening and also the intrinsic purity which is the source of both awakened Buddhas and deluded sentient beings. Forgetfulness of our lotus source has given rise to our experience of being someone real somewhere in a real world.

The wide range of prayers and practices translated and explained in this book provide guidance on how to live in a clear and ethical way. These practices ease the process of dying and guide us to Padmasambhava in his pure realm of Lotus Light, also known as Zangdopalri, the Copper Coloured Mountain.

Texts are translated by C. R. Lama and James Low.

7. The Mirror of Clear Meaning: a Commentary on the Dzogchen Treasure Text of Nuden Dorje

(Published by Simply Being, UK, 2021. ISBN: 978-1739938130)

This commentary by James Low on a traditional authentic dzogchen text by Nuden Dorje gives a clear and pithy account of how our mind actually is, cutting a clear path through the forest of our beliefs and assumptions, it brings us face to face with the presence of the radiance of our mind illuminating both its open empty ground and the ceaseless appearance of its potential. This text can be a great support for meditators and shows us how to avoid many of the mistakes and misunderstandings that can arise.

The presentation is a personal distillation of Nuden Dorje's realisation in a manner both beautiful and deeply meaningful. Short verses show with pithy clarity how the various aspects of dzogchen fit together.

This book has a conversational style, being a lightly edited transcript of teachings given by James Low in Aracena, Spain over four days in 2019.

8. Longing for Limitless Light: letting in the light of Buddha Amitabha's love

(Published by Simply Being, UK, 2021. ISBN: 978-1739938109)

This book offers a sequence of key texts in the mahayana tradition of Tibetan Buddhism. These prayers and aspirations form part of the daily practice for many in the various Tibetan Buddhist traditions. They include prayers, aspirations, rituals and descriptions of a path to enlightenment.

The loving heart of Buddha Amitabha Limitless Light invites all beings into his pure realm of Happiness known as Dewachen or Sukhavati where, say the texts, awakening is easy. Relying on the warm presence of the Enlightened Ones, our lonely struggles can be left behind as we relax into the ever-inclusive ground of our being. These practices are an effective antidote to the sense of alienation and isolation which is so pervasive at this time.

The practice texts in this book offer tried and trusted ways to connect with the buddhas whose welcome already awaits us. They include the prayers and full ritual for Taking Refuge and for Taking the Bodhisattva Vow and prayers and practices such as the Dechen Monlam for Taking Birth in Dewachen.

They provide a coherent support for developing faith and confidence in this mahayana method that unites wisdom and compassion.

Each text was translated from Tibetan by C R Lama and James Low together many years ago in India. James Low has recently revised them and written an introduction.

9. This is it: revealing the great completion

(Published by Simply Being, UK, 2021. ISBN: 978-0956923974)

Each section of the book leads into the next, showing how, by peeling away our habitual assumptions and projections, we can directly encounter the intrinsic purity of our own mind. "This is it", Dzogchen, the great completion.

The first facet, *One Thing Leads to Another,* offers sutra texts on dependent origination. The second, *Increased Transparency,* includes the Heart Sutra and indicates that all phenomena, whether seemingly outer or inner, subject or object, are empty and devoid of inherent existence.

This leads onto the third facet *Encountering the Other,* the story of how the Buddha Chakrasamvara manifested in order to deal with cruelty and malicious behaviour. The fourth Facet, *Getting Lost Invites Trouble,* offers two accounts of how pride and self-confidence can lead a person astray so that their provocations lead to a display the Buddhas' wrathful power, enforcing transformation and the abrupt end to the careers of heartless bullies.

Next, in the fifth facet, we see how transformation can be elective rather than imposed. *Cutting Free* begins with the story of Machig Labdron, her struggle to free herself from social constraints so that she could pursue a life in dharma. There is a short guru yoga practice and her Chöd practice, The Dakinis' Laughter. Finally in facet six, Just This is *The Cuckoo Cry,* the foundational text of the dzogchen mind series. In just three couplets it sets out the view, meditation and activity which are the inseparability of primordial purity and instant presence.

10. Finding Freedom: texts from the Theravadin, Mahayana and Dzogchen Buddhist traditions

(Published by Wandel Verlag, Berlin, 2019. ISBN: 978-3942380270)

This book offers three approaches to awakening. The first section, *Fighting the Good Fight,* is concerned with how we can commit ourselves to the mindful activity of renouncing our familiar and often comforting limiting habits. Here the orientation is towards leaving our familiar ego-home and going on a journey to seek something which seems only to be available elsewhere.

The second section of the book, *Mistaken Identities,* points to how we can develop the honesty and courage to face our lives as they manifest, resolving our limiting habits and releasing ourselves from misleading identities. Here the orientation is towards recognising how our self-centredness has harmed others and made us blind to our interdependency.

The third section of *Finding Freedom, Sweet Simplicity,* is concerned with how we can relax and release ourselves from all limiting habits and thus effortlessly abide in our limitless intrinsic freedom. Here the orientation is towards awakening to the actuality of our mind as it is.

These three sections are quite different in tone, yet are harmonious and compatible in their underlying message of freedom. The Buddha offered all he was to help us, and if we offer ourselves fully to the path we will awaken with the same smile he offers us.

Finding Freedom contains *The Dhammapada* by Buddha Shakyamuni, the Sharp Weapon Wheel by Dharmarakshita, and four Dzogchen texts by Tulku Tsulo, Gonpo Wangyal, Ayu Khandro and the famous Kunzang Monlam – *The Evocation of Samantabhadra*. All texts were translated from Tibetan by James Low with the guidance of C R Lama and have been revised for this book. Each section is accompanied by a comprehensive introduction that touches the depth and heart of Buddha's teaching and points to the end of sorrow for all beings and the attainment of lasting freedom.

The book has been translated into German and Polish.

11. Sparks

(Published by Simply Being, UK, 2017. ISBN: 978-0956923943)

Sparks is a wide ranging and accessible collection of short writings and poems arising from James Low's experience of practising and teaching buddhism for many years. The book's focus is on the dzogchen approach of resting in intrinsic open awareness which is the radiance of our being. In simple and beautiful language it is an expression of the profound non-dual view of dzogchen, which illuminates the enlivening buddha potential present in all of us.

Sparks' pithy collection of prose and poems can be entered at any point, enjoyed and reflected upon since each 'spark' or 'snippet' is complete in itself. The topic is profound, yet it is condensed and expressed in simple language using examples and metaphors from everyday life and the living world around us.

The book has been translated into German, Italian, Polish, Spanish and Turkish.

12. Collected Works of C. R. Lama

(Published by Simply Being, UK, 2017. ISBN: 978-0956923929)

C. R. Lama, also known as Chhimed Rigdzin Rinpoche and as Zilnon Lingpa (1922-2002), was an important lama in the Khordong and Byangter lineages of the Nyingmapa School of Tibetan Buddhism. A scholar and also a yogi, he combined these two streams in his work as

Reader in Indo-Tibetan Studies at Visva Bharati University at Santiniketan, West Bengal, India. He was a family man who was actively engaged in the world around him.

This book gathers together Rinpoche's writings on a wide range of topics including Nyingma Buddhist Philosophy, Tibetan cultural practices, his life in Khordong Monastery in Tibet and his advice for Dharma practitioners. Tulku Thondup writes, "James Low studied under the Ven. Chhimed Rigdzin Rinpoche for years with incredible dedication in austere conditions to accumulate vast knowledge of Rinpoche's teachings. This volume is filled with those precious teachings, most of which have remained unpublished until now."

The book has been translated into French, German, Polish, Spanish and Portuguese.

13. Radiant Aspiration: the Butterlamp Prayer Lamp of Aspiration
(Published by Simply Being, UK, 2011. ISBN: 978-0956923905)

This was written by C.R. Lama while in retreat in Tso Pema in India and arose as a gesture of love and longing for his teacher, Tulku Tsorlo whom he had to leave in Tibet. While alive he offered 100,000 butterlamps each year with his disciples and this practice continues.

The book offers a clear introduction to the Tibetan Buddhist understanding of the nature of existence, exploring how to free ourselves from all that limits us. It provides a translation of a beautiful prayer which employs the symbolism of the ritual offering of butterlamps, where light is seen as the basis of the non-duality of all experience. Radiant Aspiration contains the full ritual text so that readers can engage in its practice if they so choose. There is an extensive commentary focusing on the development of wisdom and compassion making the traditional text fully relevant to the modern reader.

It has been translated into German, Polish and Spanish.

14. Simply Being: Texts in the Dzogchen Tradition

(Published by Antony Rowe Publishing, UK, 2010. ISBN: 978-1907571015)

Simply Being presents twelve texts collected and translated by James Low, who copied them from the travelling libraries of yogis practising in the Himalayas.

These twelve traditional teachings show us how to recognise our own enlightened being as infinite awareness free of all effort and artifice. Freed from limiting false assumptions, human nature is revealed as a joyful process of open responsiveness.

James often teaches from the texts in this book.

This has been translated into French, German, Italian, Polish and Spanish.

15. The Seven Chapters of Prayer: as taught by Padma Sambhava of Urgyen, known in Tibetan as Le'u bDun Ma

(Published by Wandel Verlag, Berlin, 2010. ISBN: 978-3942380027)

In 1981 C R Lama wrote that *"These prayers describe how … Padma Sambhava promises to come every morning with the rising sun and to come every tenth day of the lunar month and make himself visible to the people. The prayers give protection from war, disease, famine, difficult journeys, dangerous animals, earthquakes, troublesome yeti, robbers and authoritarian police, at the time of death, during the bardo, and from the other results of one's karma."* We have also translated the Bar-Chhad Lam-Sel prayer which saves all beings in the six realms from the difficulties that afflict them. The volume concludes with the prayer listing all the important deeds of Padma Sambhava written by gTer-sTon Nyi-Ma 'Od-Zer.

These prayers are said and believed in by all the rNying-Ma lineages, only the lineage prayers at the beginning will be slightly different for the later period and here we have given the Byang-gTer, 'Khor-gDong and sMin-Grol Gling lineages. All the bKa'-brGyud-Pa also read these prayers and some of the Sa-sKya-Pa also read them, and when they do their Phur-Pa practice, they read the fourth chapter. The prayers are also read in some dGe-Lugs-Pa monasteries, and they are respected everywhere for their great blessing.

The book has been translated into French and German.

16. Being Guru Rinpoche: a Commentary on Nuden Dorje's Terma Vidyadhara Guru Sadhana

(Published by Simply Being, 2nd ed. 2022. ISBN: 978-1739938147)

Being Guru Rinpoche shows how to use a traditional Tibetan Buddhist meditation text as a method for transforming daily experience into an unbroken flow of wisdom and compassion.

It contains the tantric ritual practice called *The Vidyadhara Guru Sadhana* and James Low's brief commentary on it. The commentary is the edited transcript of two talks and in no way claims to be a complete account of the text. Rather, it is offered as a way for western people to approach the engagement with tantric practice. The text itself is from the nyingmapa tradition of Tibetan Buddhism and is a treasure text of Nuden Dorje. James first translated it with C R Lama (Chhimed Rigdzin Rinpoche) over twenty-five years ago and it has become the most frequently practised larger text amongst his students.

This ritual text is a very important one because of the depth of its content and the shortness of its lineage, in other words, its closeness to Padmasambhava, the root of all the Nyingma lineages.

This has been translated into French, German, Polish and Spanish. It is available as a Kindle e-book.

17. Being Right Here: a Dzogchen Treasure Text of Nuden Dorje Entitled the Mirror of Clear Meaning

(Published by Snow Lion, 2004. ISBN: 978-1559392082)

Being Right Here provides a very clear authentic account of the view and essential meditation of dzogchen, the practice of non-dual experience. The presentation is in the Men Ngag style, a personal instruction distilling the author's own realisation, revealing the lived experience of the terton Nuden Dorje Drophan Lingpa in a manner both beautiful and profoundly meaningful... It consists of short verses which, with pithy clarity, show how the various aspects of dzogchen fit together. The text provides both an authentic account of the practice and instruction in how to apply it.

"Giving this commentary was the last time I taught in Rinpoche's (C.R. Lama) presence and re-reading it brings back the facilitating warmth and spaciousness of his empowering and liberating display. The teacher is the site of integration; through the practice of the text the nature of life is revealed through integration with the living presence of the teacher. The teacher is of course not an entity, but a relational field," says the author.

The book has been translated into French, German, Italian, polish and portuguese.

18. The Yogins of Ladakh: a Pilgrimage Among The Hermits of The Buddhist Himalayas
(Published by Motilal Banarsidass, 1997. ISBN: 978-8120814622)

James Low wrote Chapter 15 Practising Chod in the cemeteries of Ladakh which includes a secret biography of the yogini Machig Labdron and the Chod practice which she created. It is unique to Tibetan Buddhism. *The Yogins of Ladakh* investigates the social anthropology of the area through studies of village life. Further it enquires the social organisations, history, meditational practices and philosophy of the yogins who still lived and practised in the remote parts of the area.

In the Introduction, John Crook writes, *"James Low and I undertook long journeys on foot in Ladakh to meet the yogins in their monasteries and 'caves'. Few of these yogins were teachers but they allowed us into their presence and showed us their manner of being. A landscape was set before us which we had to map as best we could. Our book is a map of the cultural landscape of these men. We hope and believe it will help Westerners both to broaden and to deep in their insight into the Dharma. Come with us then in an exploration of these inner landscapes set amongst the highest mountains of the world. It is our belief that what we found there is of great significance in the suffering world of today."*

The book has been translated into Italian.

www.ingramcontent.com/pod-product-compliance
Lightning Source LLC
Chambersburg PA
CBHW062106080426
42734CB00012B/2772